# PRIVATE LESSONS

## A VOLLEYBALL COACH'S GUIDE TO GETTING STARTED

By Whitney Bartiuk

Visit the author's website for volleyball coaches at www.getthepancake.com.

ISBN: 9798630668912

# ACKNOWLEDGMENTS

This book was written for the incredible coaches, trainers, and parents I've met while coaching and building Get The Pancake. You continuously inspire me, and I hope the favor is returned!

# TABLE OF CONTENTS

# INTRODUCTION

Hi Coach! I'm so excited that you're ready to start running private lessons. Not only will you improve the level of volleyball in your area, but you'll also be increasing the confidence of your players and building relationships within your community.

Focused attention, even in small amounts, has the potential to accelerate progress towards a goal. And that's no different in volleyball! In a typical team practice, players tend to get limited touches on the ball with occasional attention from the coach. During one-on-one sessions, athletes get in more deliberate repetitions with direct feedback. As a result, their skill level and comfort on the court skyrockets!

It doesn't matter if you're preparing an athlete for tryouts or training a group of friends to help them stand out on their club team. Private lessons are almost *always* the best way for athletes to improve their individual skills in a short amount of time.

Not only do the athletes benefit from private lessons... there's something in it for you, too!

Having gone through this several times myself, I can tell you that there is no greater experience than seeing your player's eyes light up when they finally get their first serve over the net... Or when they finally pass a tough ball into the target you've set up for them... Or when the setter and hitter you're working with really connect on a quick set for the first time... Or... okay, I think you get my point!

The personal satisfaction you get from these small victories is unreal! You get to see a lot of "firsts" when you're running lessons because you're pushing each athlete at their individual level. And if a parent or family member is there watching, it's even better! Training an athlete to jump serve is more satisfying when they nail it and look to the stands, beaming at their dad. Seeing him jump up and start cheering and clapping is the cherry on top.

By running private lessons, you also start to establish yourself in your community and build relationships. This is one of my favorite aspects of running private lessons because I've moved around a lot over the years and have coached in several states.

Coaching in a new area can be tough, especially if you have few to no connections. However, if you start offering private lessons (and you do a good job, of course), your circle will start to expand. Don't get me wrong; coaching a team is fun because you spend a lot of time with players and get to know their families a bit. But when you run private lessons, you start to understand so much more about your athletes!

What are their long-term goals? What do they struggle with the most? What is something their regular coach is teaching them, but they're too afraid to admit they don't understand?

It's fun to get to know your players, help them through their struggles, and highlight what they're doing well. What I found most interesting when I started teaching in this setting was that not everyone comes to private lessons because they want to be the star of the team! We'll expand on that throughout this book and discuss different options for lessons that will appeal to different types of players (and how to communicate well with their parents, too).

Sharing your knowledge with athletes is rewarding because of the intangibles. Feeling satisfied in their achievements after a lesson, settling into a high-level role in your community, and even just the acknowledgment from players and their families that you helped them improve… these are all great!

The benefits don't stop there. If you choose to do so, you can also make a little extra money on the side! In many areas, coaching volleyball is not the most lucrative job in the world. In fact, many coaches volunteer their time to coach local athletes (but I probably don't need to tell you that)!

Sharing your expertise in a one-on-one or small group session is much more valuable to players, who often only get generalized coaching in a team setting. Because you are providing more value to these players, you can charge more for your time.

Now, we're not out to take advantage of our position as a coach, but let's face it! Coaching is a skill that many of us have spent several years developing. While it may seem strange that players and their families are willing to pay extra for a private lesson, the value they receive for an hour of your time is likely more than you would think.

## LET'S DO THE MATH

As I mentioned, most players receive minimal individual coaching at practice when they are in a team setting. If you take your average two-hour practice and divide it by 12 players, that's only about 10-minutes per player that a coach could possibly spend with each individual! And that's if they only worked one-on-one with players. Spoiler alert: that's not how team practices work!

Even in a school setting where teams practice every

day, players still would not receive even an hour of personalized instruction in a week. Although I'm making huge generalizations here, a one-hour lesson can essentially provide players with more *individual attention* than ten hours of team practice in most instances.

Add the ability to ask "stupid" questions without fear and the fact that mistakes don't result in consequences for a team, and lessons are just about the best learning tool out there for athletes!

Team practice is, of course, needed and necessary for better performance in matches. But individual skills and a mental understanding of the game can grow exponentially when private lessons are part of an athlete's training!

To summarize, private lessons are valuable to players. As the instructor, you deserve to be compensated as such (if you desire to charge). We'll talk pricing later, so we won't worry about it for now.

Throughout these pages, I'm going to cover the basics of getting started, help you learn how to market yourself, teach you about the different types of players and parents you might run into, how to pack your schedule with private lessons, and really dig into everything you need to know about running private lessons.

I'm going to walk you through step-by-step how I would recommend you get started. Now, I guess you can jump ahead if you really want. But I think you'd be doing yourself a disservice if you skip anything in this guide.

Keep this in mind: anyone can run a private lesson once or twice. But if you want to fill your calendar with lessons week after week, I highly suggest you go through each chapter in order. Better yet, take notes along the way!

There's a lot of information in this book, and the beginning chapters primarily focus on getting started. I'll explain everything you need to do before you ever step foot on the court. Depending on your current coaching situation, you might find these steps easier or more challenging. Either way, I want to make sure you're set up for success!

Once we get the nuts and bolts out of the way, we'll cover all things on-court. The second half of the book covers topics like structuring your lesson, making adjustments if needed, and running group lessons. I even give you a small collection of drills that I use in practically every lesson I run! That's right; you don't need to reinvent the wheel. These simple (yet effective) drills can be adjusted for practically every skill level and every age.

To help you take action, I'll give you

recommendations and brief to-do lists at the end of most chapters. Running a great lesson isn't just about making your players sweat on the court (although that's a great start)! The follow-up is just as crucial to making a lasting impact on your players. If you're trying to run high-level private lessons, you'll want to complete the examples along the way!

With that, let's dive in!

# CHAPTER 1: FINDING A COURT

First things first: You need somewhere to run lessons. But finding an affordable facility with open court time is often the hardest part of getting started. I encourage you to start with this step, because the first thing a parent will want to know after asking *if* you give lessons, is *where* you give lessons.

## NO CLUB OR GYM AFFILIATION

Most schools and recreation centers do not allow individuals to run paid private lessons in their gyms or outdoor courts. If they do, you usually need to have general liability insurance that specifically names their organization as "additional insured," typically for up to $1,000,000. I've purchased my own insurance for about $350 (annual), but a quick search online shows it could go up to $600 or beyond. You'll have to investigate this for yourself, but that should give you an idea of what to expect.

Remember: Having your own insurance generally isn't required unless you're using a rental facility like a school or recreation center without a club or gym affiliation. Don't be afraid of that number. You have other options!

However, we live in a litigious society, and getting insurance for yourself might not be the worst idea. In fact, many online training courses are starting to recommend that coaches get insurance, so take that information and apply it to your situation as appropriate.

I want to be clear as we go through this training that I'm not a lawyer, insurance agent, or accountant. Remember that throughout this book! Everything is merely a suggestion and is provided to help guide you through the process of starting to run private lessons. Ultimately, it is up to you to comply with local regulations.

If you plan on using a recreation center or a school to run your private lessons, I want to make sure you know that you often can't just drop in and use the facility whenever you please. Typically, you'll need to arrange to rent out a court ahead of time.

To make a reservation, you may be required to get a permit to use the space and supply insurance information to the organization. Additionally, you may even have to go back and forth with coordinators if there's a court space issue.

This is all if you can even find the rental information in the first place. I don't know why, but many organizations make it very challenging to find rental details and documents on their websites. Additionally, front desk staff will rarely know the process to rent out space if you call in to ask.

As you can tell, finding court space and renting it is generally a complicated process. You will need to get permits, schedule lessons far in advance, and coordinate with facility staff. This is in addition to tracking down the rental information to begin with. Seriously. I'd like to challenge you to find the rental process for gym space in your local area. It's tough!

For this reason, I highly recommend that you become affiliated with a club volleyball program, even if your only purpose will be to join the staff as a coach who runs private lessons. In my experience, this isn't very common yet, but I have a feeling that this is going to become more and more popular as coaches realize the opportunities they're missing out on by not working with a club.

## CURRENT CLUB OR GYM AFFILIATION

There will still be costs and requirements for you to run lessons out of a club, but in my experience, this is much easier to do and has the potential to save you a lot on court fees and extra insurance. Not only could you potentially save a ton of money, but you will likely have more access to interested families, and the headache of scheduling lessons will be significantly reduced.

If you already work for a club but they don't run private lessons yet, meet with the Director to discuss getting this started. If this is new for the club, here are a few topics you'll want to cover with your Director:

- Court rental fees for coaches

- Lesson rates

- Court availability

- The scheduling process

- Insurance coverage

Hopefully you've got an idea about where you're going to run your private lessons. The following to-do list offers a quick recap of steps to take before moving forward towards running private lessons.

# CHAPTER 1 TO-DO LIST:

<u>Not Affiliated With A Club</u>:

- Compare court costs of local recreation centers, schools, and gyms.

- Reach out to club programs to see if they would hire you to run private lessons.

- Decide which scenario is best for you (i.e., lowest cost, closest to home, etc.).

- Complete any paperwork to rent space if needed (i.e., rental forms, insurance, permits, etc.).

<u>Affiliated With A Club That Does Not Offer Private Lessons</u>:

- Schedule a meeting with your Director.

- Share your interest in running private lessons through the club.

- Discuss the topics of court rental fees for coaches, lesson rates, court availability, the scheduling and registration processes, and payment process.

<u>Affiliated With A Club That Offers Private Lessons</u>:

What are you waiting for? As soon as you finish this book, tell your Director that you want to run lessons!

# CHAPTER 2: SAFETY

I'm going to be real with you…

CPR/AED and First Aid certifications are not optional. If you coach somewhere that does not require these certifications, I'd honestly turn and run the other way. If you're going to be coaching children or working with them on a court, you need to have the fundamental knowledge that comes with this training.

There *will* come a time when you need it! And the last thing you want to do in an emergency is panic, or worse yet, cause an athlete further harm due to your misinformed attempts to take care of them.

Over the years, I've had to deal with mostly sprained ankles, cuts, and bloody noses. But I've also dealt with heat-related illnesses (which have the potential to be life-threatening) and know of situations that happened involving "agonal breathing." If you've never heard of agonal breathing before, it's when someone is in cardiac arrest and looks like they're breathing somewhat normally, but they are not. If you see this but don't know what's happening, it means someone who needs medical attention may not receive it.

There are a lot of scenarios you need to be prepared for when coaching. I'm going to elaborate on my own experiences to help you understand the importance of your safety training (and why you need to pay attention, too).

I'd like to highlight that in these situations, I wasn't the only adult around. However, I was the only one who noticed the signs and reacted!

The first time I faced a potential medical issue was during a summer camp for a high school. It was pretty hot outside, but we were in an air-conditioned gym. We started for the day and ran through a warm-up and maybe a drill or two before taking our first water break. As players hustled off the court, I noticed that one of the players was hanging back and walking very slowly towards the hallway.

The best way I can describe what drew my attention to her was that she just looked a little "off." Because of this, I went over to her and asked if she was feeling okay. She didn't look me in the eyes and was staring off into space. She told me she felt "a little dizzy" and that she was "seeing spots."

Keep in mind, I had never dealt with anything more severe than a sprained ankle at this point, and the idea of a heat-related illness never crossed my mind as we were in an air-conditioned gym.

I put my hand around her back and started guiding her towards the drinking fountain outside the gym. As we were made our way through the double doors to the hallway, she dropped to the floor.

I will tell you right now… it is a terrifying experience to have a 14-year-old collapse in front of you.

Thankfully, I was walking with her and already steadying her as we went. I felt her knees give out before I actually saw it, and was able to catch her as she fell to the ground. Even though she was relatively small, I nearly fell on top of her from her dead weight.

To this day, that's the scariest moment that I've ever experienced coaching: feeling a player crumple towards the ground as I tried to soften her impact on the floor. All while trying not to fall myself, or let her head bounce off the door frame or ground.

Now, she didn't lose consciousness, but she definitely was not able to hold herself up. Heatstroke, heat exhaustion, and all those other things that you learn about... You never know when you're going to need to remember your training.

I vividly remember other coaches (in my sport and others) who were around when this happened. They were just as shocked as I was, but they didn't know what to do. Unfortunately, the athletic trainer was not in their office, either.

I was the only coach who had paid attention during the training and knew the signs pointed to this being a heat-related illness. In these situations, sometimes you need to call the ambulance. This time we just needed to cool her down. She ended up being fine and coming back the next day after a doctor visit, but it could have been a big deal. Because I had paid attention during my training, I knew what to do in the situation.

Not only did my education help in the moment. I also noticed she was "off" and knew to go to her to make sure she was alright. Imagine if she had fainted on the court and hurt herself. Or maybe she would have gotten to the same point and hit her head on the hallway tiles or the door frame...

I don't know what would have happened, but it probably would have been a lot worse if I hadn't noticed her in the first place.

The second time I noticed a player moving sluggishly, we were outside during a private lesson. Although we had scheduled to play early in the morning to avoid high temperatures, I noticed this player moving very slow. We hadn't done anything too exhausting up until that point, yet she was having difficulty talking to me. Because I knew the heat could be getting to her, I forced her to take a long water break in the shade (despite her saying she was ready to play again).

Players will often try to play through injuries and when they're not feeling well, simply to keep the coach "happy." This player later said she didn't want to disappoint me by being "weak" and asking for a break. It was clear that she wasn't feeling well, and out of extreme caution, I ended the lesson. I did not want a repeat of my past experience!

While I spoke with the mother about how we'd hold the lesson another day, the player ended up vomiting in the bushes. Whatever doubt there was that this was a heat issue disappeared. I promptly sent them home and suggested immediate cold air conditioning in the car and a cold shower once they got back.

Many other coaches I've worked with have also experienced serious injuries with their players. If you haven't yet, it's only a matter of time.

Don't expect other people to know how to act. If a

player collapses or you hear a loud \*pop\* and see a player drop to the ground, you need to be ready to deal with it. CPR/AED/First Aid certifications are usually required for insurance coverage and to be a coach, but really... please pay attention to the training itself.

In addition to receiving training and your certifications, I recommend you download "cheat sheets" to help you in an emergency. There are plenty of helpful charts (be sure they're from official health organizations) to help you determine what you're dealing with in stressful situations.

I've listed where to find CPR/AED/First Aid classes near you, as well as a chart from the Centers for Disease Control and Prevention on determining the difference between Heat Exhaustion and Heatstroke.

One final thought on credentials... the likelihood that you need to use this training is pretty small. I'm sorry if I scared you! But I want to make sure you understand how important it is to be prepared! Most of the time, you'll be on the court laughing and having a great time. But the one day that you need this information, I want you to be ready.

# CHAPTER 2 TO-DO LIST:

- Find CPR/AED/First Aid classes near you: https://www.redcross.org/take-a-class/first-aid

- Print helpful PDF from the CDC on Heat-Related Illnesses: https://www.cdc.gov/disasters/extremeheat/pdf/Heat_Related_Illness.pdf

# CHAPTER 3: TRACKING INCOME AND EXPENSES

How you receive payment for your lessons will impact the reporting you need to do when tax time rolls around.

I know, it stinks, but... you've got to pay your taxes!

How you'll pay them, I'm not here to answer. Remember that whole part at the beginning of the book about me not being a tax professional?

If you receive a W-2 from your organization for running lessons, go ahead and skip this section! If you're an independent contractor or just coaching on your own, there are certain things you should track when it comes to running private lessons.

In my experience, most coaches will arrange their own lessons as independent contractors, and for that reason, they need to track income. If you want the chance to save yourself some money on taxes, you should also track expenses like mileage and equipment costs.

I've included a link to the IRS website at the end of this chapter. It lists business expenses you can deduct if you are self-employed or a 1099 independent contractor (which is how most coaches are classified in my experience). However, you *must* check this information with your tax professional as tax laws change all the time.

A few items you should track expenses for include:

- Mileage (there are many apps for separating personal and business drives, which you'll need to do).

- Equipment costs (cones, whistles, ball carts, boxes, etc., if you purchase them yourself for coaching purposes).

- Clothing costs (specialized coaching clothes can often be included in business expenses). Unfortunately, you can't go on a legging shopping spree and add them unless you only use them during coaching.

- Court rental fees.

- General Liability Insurance for coaching (if not provided by your school or club program, or the gym you work with).

A full list of potential business expenses from the IRS can be found at the url noted at the end of this chapter.

Keeping track of this can get messy (or even lost), so I suggest using a spreadsheet available in the cloud or some other spreadsheet online that you can access whenever you need it. This way, you can update as you go and never forget to add a lesson or expense!

Using an online tracker also helps you when it comes time to file taxes because you can typically export your data into one organized spreadsheet. Pen and paper are fine, but I like the ease of digital tracking.

I highly recommend you make it a habit to track income and expenses as they occur. If you don't do it along the way, it's going to become unorganized. Meaning you will probably lose out on some money!

## THREE WAYS TO TRACK YOUR INCOME

The first is pretty simple, and that's using pen and paper. If you like to plan your private lessons in a notebook, it's simple to have a section for income and expenses and to track everything there.

The second method is to track your money using a note-taking app on your phone or an online spreadsheet that you can access from anywhere. I don't think anyone leaves the house without their phone anymore, so this allows you to always have access to your information.

Using these basic applications will help keep track of purchases. Like when you go to the store and buy some new shoes just for coaching! All you need to do is open that document on your phone and make a note of your purchase. For even better accuracy/proof of your purchases, snap a photo of your receipt and store it on your phone!

My last suggestion for you is going to be to use specialized apps. There are many apps out there that help you track income and expenses, and apps that help monitor your mileage, too!

If you use note-taking apps or cloud-based programs to create documents for work and your personal life, it could be easy to lose your private lesson documents. For this reason, I recommend using apps dedicated to tracking income and expenses for private lessons.

# CHAPTER 3 TO-DO LIST:

- Check for applicable deductions here: https://www.irs.gov/businesses/small-businesses-self-employed/deducting-business-expenses

- Track income and expenses in the cloud: https://www.google.com/drive

- Find apps to help you track your income and expenses. I like the app "Dollarbird" for everything except driving expenses, and "MileIQ" has worked well for me in the past to track mileage.

# CHAPTER 4: EQUIPMENT

Before you start running lessons, you might need to invest in some equipment.

Don't worry; you can run plenty of lessons with just a net and a full ball cart! But I'm going to share a secret with you…

The more equipment you use in a private lesson, the more valuable it will seem to the player and the parent. This is because it will look more specialized (it is), and players don't often get to use extra equipment in typical practices.

By getting out a setter target or floor markers, we're typically training players better because we're using training tools and equipment specific to each skill.

I'll point out my personal favorite (i.e., the one that I think makes the most significant impact), but players and parents tend to think certain training tools are more valuable than others. Regardless of monetary value, using any of the following equipment is sure to level up your coaching.

Here's a rundown of the tools and equipment I've found add the most value to lessons, from the most basic to the tools that players and parents like the most.

# A WATCH

You don't need to have a smartwatch or even a timer on your watch. But I can tell you this… you do not want to use your phone to keep track of the time! Honestly, if you've got your phone out at all during the lesson, you're probably going to have a negative impact on the lesson.

Having a watch allows you to keep track of time without looking like you're texting in the middle of the lesson (whether you are or not, no one knows). I'm not going to lie to you. I've forgotten my watch on a handful of occasions and had to use my phone to check the time. Despite your best intentions, if you have a notification that pops up when you check the time, you *will* get distracted by the banner floating on your screen.

This brief pause where you read and evaluate what is on the phone makes players feel like you're not engaged, and parents will likely feel the same way. So, leave your phone in your backpack or purse, and remember to charge your watch before it's time to head to your next lesson!

## CONES

These are another basic, and you can get a set of 10 for less than $10 at most stores that carry sporting goods equipment. I actually found a good deal on some fun colored ones at a large discount department store, so the next time you're in one, just poke around in the sporting goods aisle.

Your gym might also have cones you can use, so you could save a little money in the beginning by using their equipment. However... this is another purchase (like the watch) that I recommend to everyone when they're getting started. I enjoy having my own cones because I know for sure that I'll have them. This helps me plan my lessons better.

Using cones gives better feedback to players and parents and can help motivate players better than just saying, "hit to that corner" or "serve to that zone."

Outlining the target gives your players clear feedback on whether they hit the zone or not, and even helps clarify abstract ideas like "deep" and "short" for newer players.

One drawback to cones is that if they get hit by a ball or stepped on, they'll likely go flying. For this reason, I avoid using cones to show players where to step. I don't want them to slip and get injured!

## FLOOR MARKERS

I haven't had a lesson yet where a player didn't say, "Oooh, those are cool!" when I got out the floor markers. A step up from cones, floor markers are flat, slip-resistant circles that help you show players where to stand or how to move on the court without interfering in play.

Players can step on them, so they are great for mapping out footwork patterns or creating boundaries on the court. Make sure your floor is clean, so they actually stick to the surface! While I don't map out footwork patterns with my team because everyone's steps are different, in lessons, you can be more exact and tailor the placement to your player.

I use circular markers in different colors to show different patterns (i.e., blue is left foot, red is right foot, etc.) but there are really cool ones out there that are shaped like a foot, ones that are in line and corner shapes, and some even have numbers printed on them.

In my opinion, you can't go wrong with basic colored dots, so I'd recommend you start there. While your players will think they're neat, I think the greatest benefit is for the coach who can explain things easier and quicker, helping the player learn faster. I'm going to say this is the best "bang-for-your-buck" piece of equipment.

## TABLET

I already said not to have your phone out. Why would I suggest you bring a tablet? Using slow-mo is one of the easiest ways for YOU to find an issue with a player's form when you can't tell what's going on in real-time.

Sometimes it's just the tiniest tweak that will make the biggest difference, and our eyes can't always see it as it's happening. I recommend a tablet because it has a larger screen, allowing you to show video feedback to your player comfortably. Remember: Don't film anyone without permission from both the player and the parent or guardian.

Asking for permission in-person is fine, but I would prefer to have it in writing that it's okay to use film as a teaching tool. And do not post or share your videos without permission. Sure, plenty of people share pictures and videos of their kids all over the internet, and maybe you have a cool video from a lesson you want to share on your account.

But there are plenty of parents who don't want videos of their kids on the internet, which coaches need to respect.

If you are going to use a tablet for lessons, I would recommend that you only use it for volleyball specifically. Scrolling through videos of your player and then accidentally swiping too far to a picture of you and your friends on a girls trip in Vegas doesn't exactly scream "professional."

To recap:

- Get permission from the parents (preferably in writing) before you use video to help their child.

- Don't share the video unless you have clear communication in writing that it is okay.

- Use your tablet for volleyball only.

If you're going to use a tablet, I also recommend investing in a tripod and a tablet-holding attachment. This allows you to film handsfree, giving you greater flexibility during a lesson.

## BOXES

If you played volleyball when you were younger, think about how excited you got when you saw the boxes out at practice... nothing has changed! Kids still love the boxes!

They want to sit on them, stand on them, jump on and off of them, and even curl up in a ball and take a nap on top. Boxes are an excellent training tool for a couple of skills (mainly hitting and blocking), but they're used best when teaching fundamentals or breaking down a skill into small parts.

Working on arm swing is one example, or learning how a block should feel. You probably will not use boxes that frequently, so this piece of equipment is more "nice to have" rather than a necessity. But players and parents seem to think this is an outstanding training tool!

Additionally, you can use boxes while working with passers (so you can get up high and hit at them) and servers (giving them a big target to aim for). I personally believe they are more beneficial to the lesson because of the options it provides the coach rather than the situations it allows you to put players in.

You can either buy one (there are even collapsible ones available) or build your own. I occasionally see plans online for volleyball boxes, so if you or a friend is competent enough to construct one, this could be a great way to save some money.

I'm sure this goes without saying, but ensure that the boxes are safe before you use them. This means sturdy, not sharp, padded, and balanced. A wider box is better for more situations, and wheels on one side of each box help move these monsters around the gym.

Boxes are notorious for scratching gym floors, so be sure to have a clear plan for moving them without damaging the court. You want to make money, not spend it resurfacing someone else's gym floor!

## PASSING AND SETTING TARGETS

Alright... I saved the best for last! I'm still trying to find the right mix of how often to use these with long-term lessons because, honestly, I would love to use them every session. But I also don't want them to lose their magic! If you want your athletes to think you are the coolest coach, and love taking lessons with you, invest in a passing or setting target. Better yet, convince your Director to purchase a couple. Then you can use them without paying for them yourself!

I love these things because you will see tremendous growth, often in one lesson. Players of all ages get so excited when they pass the ball or set the ball into a small target, and I have found they are one of the biggest motivators for players to develop their skills!

Another benefit of using targets is how it improves parents' understanding of the game. A lot of parents did not grow up playing volleyball, and I am always asked questions by club and high school parents about rules, strategies, and tactics when I'm in a crowd.

Unless parents played volleyball when they were younger, they probably have no idea what's going on. Using a target lets the parents know how good (or poorly) their child is doing in their attempt to pass or set the ball. Again, we're taking something abstract ("pass it here at about this height," while waving our arms around) and making it much clearer (pass it into this hoop).

## CHAPTER 4 TO-DO LIST:

- Find links to suggested equipment for coaches at:

  www.amazon.com/shop/getthepancake

# CHAPTER 5: KNOW YOUR VALUE

It's finally time to start talking about getting yourself some lessons!

But before we dive into marketing strategies and different approaches you can take to get those lessons, I want to share something with you about your mindset.

And that is... it's okay to make money from teaching volleyball. Now, you don't have to charge if you don't want to. I know plenty of coaches who are willing and able to donate their time to help kids in their community get better at volleyball. Tons of coaches want to help their athletes succeed, and only charge players enough to cover their costs. However, I've found that these coaches often only consider court rental fees but not additional expenses they may incur like gas, certifications, time spent, etc.

That's fine. And honestly, the world is a better place

because there are people able to donate their time and expertise in that way.

However, for most of us coaches, that is not sustainable. While I love coaching, it does take time away from family and other activities where I could be making money (those student loans aren't going to pay themselves). So, I'm just going to say it how it is… my time is valuable. And yours is, too!

Over the years, I've gotten to know a lot of coaches through my website, www.getthepancake.com. I know that many of us are quick to question ourselves, our abilities, and our worth. I want to make sure you're not undervaluing yourself just because the "common" knowledge is that youth sports coaches "shouldn't" get paid.

I love it that plenty of coaches out there can volunteer their time and teach players without asking for payment in return. But I am not in that position yet (although hopefully someday I will be). At this point, I run lessons with the intention of making money doing something I love and that I am highly skilled at.

In the next chapter, we're going to talk about pricing. Before we get there, though, I want to make sure you know that it's okay to make money coaching volleyball. And not just a couple of bucks, either!

While I was living in an area where volleyball lessons were highly sought after, I was able to quit my full-time job to coach volleyball "full-time." I put that in quotations because I worked about half as many hours in a week, with much less stress, and earned roughly the same amount of money. Not bad, right?

I'm currently in a location where lessons aren't as popular, but I intend to grow my private lesson base and get back to similar levels as time and space allow at my gym.

If you've never run private lessons before, this may come as a shock to you... but it's possible to make over $100 per hour. Regularly! If your goal is to make money running private lessons, help athletes improve, and coach in a sport you love, I'm going to share some tips to optimize your income while providing a unique service for your community.

If you're fortunate enough to want to focus more on running great lessons without charging your players the market value of a lesson, that's fine too! This entire book is dedicated to running high-level lessons with a variety of players and setting you up for success no matter what you intend to charge.

Knowing your value is an important topic, though. Coaching volleyball has long been associated with low pay and dependent on kind-hearted people who were willing and able to donate their time.

Coaching volleyball is fun, it gets you moving around, and there many more benefits associated with coaching volleyball. For many of us, it can even feel bad to accept any money for doing something we love so much.

In my first coaching job, I actually lost money because of the amount of gas I used to get to and from practices and tournaments!

So, before we get into sales pitches and the nitty-gritty parts of finding athletes to work with, I need you to understand that it is okay, no... perfectly normal, to ask for money in return for a valuable service.

Players and parents will sign up for lessons with you for various reasons (which we'll get to later), but the overarching reason is that they see a skill deficiency somewhere, and they believe you can fix it!

Depending on your geographical area, playing and coaching experience, costs associated with giving lessons, and the level of players you're aiming to work with, you'll have to play around with your price point. But whatever you're initially thinking is probably lower than what the market value is.

Don't worry; we'll discuss all this stuff later in greater detail. But you need to be in the right mindset before we get there.

I want you to keep these four things in mind before we move on:

- Coaches *can* make money teaching skills and strategies to young athletes.

- Coaches *should* get paid for sharing valuable information that others cannot get without a coach.

- Coaches *do* get paid over $100 an hour for private lessons.

- Coaches *should not* feel guilty charging money for something of value which is in demand.

Remember: For most of us, coaching wouldn't be in our lives if we weren't able to afford it. If you can make a living (or a decent amount on the side) from coaching, it's much more likely that you'll stay "in the game."

By keeping coaches *coaching*, we increase the quality of instruction our players receive and improve their experience, which is really what coaching is all about!

# CHAPTER 6: PRICING

Before we can decide on a price that's right for you, let's talk about a few things you need to consider first.

Pricing mainly comes down to costs and the value of your time.

If you followed along with the chapter on income and expenses, you know what to count as expenses. But now we need to estimate how much each lesson will end up costing us. I've put together a list of typical costs most coaches will encounter while running private lessons.

## TRANSPORTATION COSTS

You most likely need to travel to get to your lesson. Depending on gas prices in your area, the gas mileage of your vehicle, potential parking charges, and your proximity to where you'll be giving lessons, transportation costs can vary wildly. You're also using your car, so there's a hidden cost there as well. I estimate that my travel expenses are between $5-$10 for travel to each lesson I regularly give within a 15-mile radius. You know your situation better than me, so sit down and calculate how much you think you'll spend traveling to the average lesson.

## COURT RENTALS

You'll probably have to pay for court time unless you are the owner of a facility. Even then, there are costs associated with using the court in place of another activity. I've paid $20 for half a court, $25 for a full-court (different clubs/areas), but I know court costs can quickly go upwards of $50 an hour (mainly through schools and recreation center rentals). Find out this information before you quote someone on the price of a lesson with you!

## EQUIPMENT COSTS

Equipment probably won't cost you too much if you're able to use volleyballs and ball carts as part of your court rental. However, if you need to buy your own, this will be a pretty significant cost upfront. Decent practice volleyballs run about $30 each, and carts can go up to $150.

I'd say ten volleyballs are the minimum you'll want

before you can run a lesson efficiently, but more would be better. I've made lessons work with only three volleyballs, but there are a ton of limitations with less. Try your hardest to avoid buying your own. You should also consider the costs of other equipment like cones, targets, whistles, etc. Draft out a sample private lesson and see what you prefer to use to get an idea of potential equipment costs.

## TAXES

Remember: You will have to pay taxes, even if it's not right now. Calculate what percentage will likely go to taxes and expect that as an expense since you will not be keeping that portion in the long run.

## WHAT YOUR TIME IS WORTH

Alright, so now that we have expenses planned out, it's time to figure out what your time is worth.

If you have coached before, this should be relatively simple. You were either paid hourly (and therefore can easily see what an hour of your time was valued at by your employer) or received a stipend and can divide that monthly total by your hours worked to find an hourly wage.

If you haven't coached before, look up coaching jobs in your area, or in areas similar to yours if there are no jobs posted in your city. Examples of hourly pay I was able to find online range from $12.50 to $40 an hour. If you're brand new to coaching, expect to be on the lower end of that range.

While some coaches only make minimum wage when they first start coaching, I do not suggest charging such a low number for your time. That may be what your time is worth managing a team, but one-on-one, you provide more value to each family. Your rate for lessons should be higher than when you coach a team.

Club or school ranking and coaching experience also create a perception of value for parents and family members who pay for these lessons. A useful guide on where to price your time could start with an analysis of what similar coaches and clubs charge. Adjust up or down depending on what the demand is like in your area.

For example, my club was charging $40 per hour for lessons in the greater Chicago area, and we were a middle-of-the-pack club. That rate was slightly below the price of $60 per hour the top clubs were charging. I was paid $20 per hour out of that $40 after all of the expenses were accounted for.

When I lived in the Dallas, Texas area, the demand for private lessons was much higher. Even though I was still at a club where we were in the middle of our region's rankings, I charged $85 per hour. After my expenses, I would leave with about $55 for a one-on-one lesson. Location matters and will probably have the largest influence on your final price.

There are going to be some other factors to consider when we get to group lessons. When working with a small group, there's a different type of pay structure that reduces the cost per player, while bumping up your take-home pay. We'll get to that later in the book when we talk specifically about running group lessons.

If you still really, honestly, have no idea what your time is worth, I would recommend charging no less than $20-$25 per hour after expenses. To simplify the math here, just take what you're going to pay for your rental and gas costs, then add your rate on top of that.

# CHAPTER 6 TO-DO LIST:

Research prices for comparable clubs and coaches in your area. Based on your experience and ranking in relation to these places and coaches, identify the price you feel most comfortable charging.

Examples of one-on-one private lesson prices (not take-home pay) I found listed online in select areas of the United States:

- Teams in the Midwest: $50-$80 per hour.

- Teams in the South: $45-$85 per hour.

- Teams in the West: $50-$80 per hour.

- Teams in the Northeast: $60-$75 per hour.

- Top listed rate found: $100 per hour in Los Angeles, California.

- Lowest listed rate found: $25 per hour in Northwest Idaho.

*These are all examples and may differ in your area. For a list of club programs nearby, you can go to USA Volleyball's website and look through club teams by region: https://www.teamusa.org/usa-volleyball/membership/regions.

Once you've found a club that you think is similar to yours or is in a nearby area, look for "Private

Lessons," "Lessons," or "Training" on most club websites to find information on their private lessons. Occasionally clubs will keep this information private, but if you check three or four websites, you should be able to find some rates.

Remember, most coaches wrongly assume they should be paid less than what the market will actually tolerate. If you are attempting to make a profit on your time invested in coaching private lessons, I recommend charging no less than $20-$25 per hour on top of expenses for a one-on-one lesson.

# CHAPTER 7: MARKETING TECHNIQUES

It's time to start yelling it from the rooftops… you're in business! To help you get started, I'm going to share a few simple "marketing" opportunities with you. Some are easier than others, but I highly encourage you to try them all out, at least once!

## POST YOUR AVAILABILITY ONLINE

Depending on how into social media you are, this may or may not have a wide reach. One way you can get your posts in front of more people is to make sure your posts are public. This makes it so your friends can share your posts, potentially helping you reach a broader audience!

My personal favorite is Facebook, but I'm sure this will evolve and change over time. People regularly go on this platform seeking recommendations, making it the perfect place to share what you're doing. Friends are often happy to share your posts if it might help someone on their friend list. It's up to you if you want to post the price you're charging, but usually just saying that you're offering volleyball lessons will elicit a few responses on its own.

Here are a couple of example posts you're free to copy and use for yourself:

Example #1:

If your friend list lacks potential clients:

*"Hey friends, I've been coaching volleyball for (x # of seasons/years), and I've finally decided to offer private lessons! All lessons will be at (gym name), and I currently have 6:00pm-8:00pm open on Monday and Wednesday nights. If you know someone who might be interested, please share this with them and have them message me for more info!"*

Example #2:

If you're well known in the area and have many people on your friend list who would be interested:

*Starting next week, I'm going to offer one-hour private volleyball lessons at (gym name) from 3:00pm-6:00pm! Let me know if you want to sign your child up. I only have a few slots available, and it's first-come, first-served! Message me for more information.*

Leave your posts up and maybe even post a few reminders. With how busy everyone is these days, it's likely that a friend may not see your first (or even second) post the next time they log on. Have patience, and know that this is only one way for you to try to arrange lessons

## TELL YOUR FRIENDS AND FAMILY

I can't begin to tell you how many people know I'm a volleyball coach because I told my Grandma about it. She then goes to the senior center and tells her friends. If they have granddaughters who play volleyball, and if they're interested in lessons, this increases the chances that they would be able to contact me.

It's the same with friends and coworkers (especially if they have kids of their own who you could coach). You may be running lessons to make money, but if you want to get a couple of low-pressure lessons under your belt before you start marketing outside of your friend group, you could offer a discount to those closest to you.

## LET YOUR DIRECTOR KNOW

If you're in a club environment, your Director should already know if you're running lessons or not! But we're going to take it a step further and make sure they know that you're actively seeking *more* lessons.

Directors are often approached for lessons simply because they're the Director. Families will assume that this is the person most qualified to give lessons at the club (which may or may not be true). However, Directors often have a lot on their plates. Even if they want to give lessons, there's usually no time for them to do so.

If your Director knows that you are actively seeking new athletes to work with, they'll likely recommend families contact you to set something up. This is even if other coaches at your club offer lessons!

Directors are generally very helpful people, and while they'll want to make sure you're a good fit for the player in question before recommending you, they'll try to help you out if they know you're a good match.

In addition to letting your Director know that you're looking for players to give lessons to, let other coaches know as well. They can often be one of your best referral sources!

There have been plenty of times in the past when I was offering lessons, but my schedule didn't match up with a family, or their location was a little too far out of my travel range. Instead of just telling them "no" and sending them on their way, I recommended other coaches who I thought might be available and would be a good fit.

Likewise, coaches have sent me players that they didn't match up with for whatever reason, and this boosted the number of lessons I regularly gave per week. Communication creates a great environment for coaches to work in and helps families match up with a coach that best fits their needs.

## JUST ASK FOR THE LESSON

Possibly one of the most challenging (yet extremely simple) ways to organize a lesson with a player is to straight up ask their parent. If I think someone could benefit from a private lesson, asking their family if they're interested almost always results in a yes, or at least a maybe!

One of the hardest parts about this, particularly if you're uncomfortable with "sales," is getting over your fear of asking in the first place. But think about it. You're asking to work one-on-one with someone because you just *know* that if you had an hour to go over the things they're struggling with, it could make a huge difference in how they play!

Personally, I tend to see big improvements from most players after about three or four one-hour lessons.

But if a player struggles with something basic like their overhand serve or they're confused by their approach footwork, you can see big changes in their performance (and confidence level) after just one session.

Plus, if you follow the tips presented in this book, they'll continue to benefit from your lesson even after they step off the court.

## BUILDING YOUR CLIENT LIST

I recommend that you only give paid private lessons to players who are not on your team. When you're putting in extra time with individual players, you could run into several issues.

First, players will typically improve through private lessons. If you have a player who improves so much that they go from being a sub to a starter, for example, you could be accused of playing favorites. Other players and parents might suggest that this player is only getting more playing time because they're paying more for private lessons, without considering improved skills.

Additionally, even if a player is taking lessons with you, this does not guarantee that they will improve enough to earn more playing time on your team. You then end up with frustrated parents who feel that you're just charging them with no real payoff for their child. Even though you might be able to see a player has developed and gotten better, parents typically measure improvement based on increases in playing time.

For these reasons, I send my players to other coaches for private lessons (unless we're out of season). So... who's left to work with?

One of the easiest ways to meet prospective families is to work during camps and clinics with a local club. You will meet players who are interested in improvement, and this could be a great way to get to know a family before you commit to running lessons with them.

Getting to know your players and their families is another way to find lessons because you could offer one of your time slots to a younger (or older) sibling.

Let's say you finally decide you want to ask someone for a lesson. What do you say? I've found that approaching parents with specific talking points really helps keep the conversation light and flowing.

In the next chapter, you'll learn how to promote yourself in-person, whether you know the parents or not.

# CHAPTER 7 TO-DO LIST:

- Post your availability online using one of the examples listed in this chapter.

- Tell your friends and family you're offering lessons the next time you see them.

- Let your Director and other coaches in your organization know that you're starting to offer private lessons. They may have some suggestions if they know you're looking for athletes to work with!

- Think of three people you know that you could ask to sign up for lessons.

# CHAPTER 8: PROMOTING YOURSELF IN-PERSON

When you are trying to find players to work with, you will find out quickly that parents want to hear about your experience. Put bluntly; parents will want to know, "what makes you worth the money?"

## TALK THE TALK

It will be good practice for you to sit down and think up an "elevator pitch" for yourself. If you've never heard of an elevator pitch before, it is essentially a short speech intended to inform your audience in the time it would take to ride an elevator with them. Ideally, this brief introduction takes about 30-seconds, but up to one-minute is generally considered an elevator pitch.

I'll give you an example of an elevator pitch, and then I'll break down how you can come up with your own.

# MY ELEVATOR PITCH

*"I've been coaching for over a decade and have worked with players from five-years-old to 18. My favorite age to coach is 14 and under because that is when players progress beyond the basics and can start working on tactics and strategies. Having coached for so long, I have a good sense of what other coaches are looking for. I enjoy pushing players at their personal limit and work with families to help their athletes achieve the goals they set for themselves."*

Now, you won't always be asked directly, "why should we take lessons with you?" In fact, you may not always give your practiced elevator pitch in one go. Instead, what will most likely happen is you'll weave your pitch throughout a conversation.

To keep this conversation flowing, it is essential to know your strengths.

Depending on your personality and confidence in your coaching abilities, this may be tough. I'm very confident in my coaching abilities because I've been doing it for so long. But even when I first started giving lessons, I was nervous and worried that I wasn't actually good enough to give lessons!

If you are mentally tougher than me and don't need a pep talk, go ahead and skip this short list. But otherwise, let me tell you why you are most likely capable of running a great volleyball lesson:

- *You care.* Clearly! You're doing your research, planning ahead, and you obviously want to give lessons. That's already a great start!

- The first time you try something new, it's going to be difficult. But you *will* get better once you experience it and know what to expect.

- Every coach has something to contribute to the sport. You may be a great setter and can pass that knowledge on to high schoolers. Or you might be extremely motivational, and you'll find players who need someone to believe in them. You don't have to be great at *everything* to give lessons. Find an area you excel in and focus on building a client list from that.

Okay. Pep talk over.

Now let's talk about your strengths.

## DEFINING YOUR STRENGTHS

Strengths can be related to years of experience playing or coaching, knowledge of certain positions, how you work with a particular age group, training outside of volleyball (physical therapists, for example), or any number of things.

Here's a list of my strengths:

- Began coaching in 2008 and have worked with athletes of practically every age in most volleyball settings.

- Work especially well with 12u-14u players.

- Able to explain confusing concepts and lead players through progressions.

- Teach strategy while I'm teaching skills.

- I'm positive.

And I can stop there!

Some of the coaches I've worked with in the past had these strengths:

- Personal trainer certification.

- Doctor of Physical Therapy.

- Played in college.

- Played for a large club and won National Championships.

- Played for a small club that was very resourceful.

- Well-connected in the coaching world, and always knew about new coaching trends and strategies that were emerging.

- From a different country and brought a different perspective into their coaching.

- Had coached for over 20 years.

- Were fresh out of college and had recent playing experience.

Literally, just think about why you are *different* from other coaches, and you're all set! Now, put those strengths into one or two short paragraphs, and you've got yourself an elevator pitch!

## WALK THE WALK

If you're heading to the gym or out and about where you might run into athletes or their parents, wear volleyball coaching gear.

When I walk into a gym where a volleyball match or tournament is going on, and I'm wearing my coaching gear, a parent typically approaches me. This could be to ask a quick question about what's happening in the match, but I've been asked about giving lessons… even when I had never met the person!

Of course, this doesn't always happen, but you're much more likely to stand out. Even better if you're by yourself because then people will be more likely to approach you.

If you do attend a local match and you're looking for lessons, strike up a conversation with parents about how well their daughter (or son) is doing. Point out one or two technical things they are doing well, and most parents will immediately become more interested in speaking with you.

If a parent asks what they could do better, you could point out a small change they could make. "I noticed she's dropping her elbow on her serve. If she could keep it up high, she'd have more power.

This feedback is informative and helpful, and you're not asking for anything… yet! You're showing this parent (and anyone within earshot) that you are competent and knowledgeable. You can then point out other players who are doing it well so the parent has a visual understanding of what you're saying, not just a verbal description.

Pointing out other players who are doing well could also spur new conversations with that player's parents if they are nearby. You may or may not get a lesson by going and watching a local match or tournament. Still, by increasing your visibility in the volleyball community, you are increasing your chances.

# CHAPTER 8 TO-DO LIST:

- List five strengths that you have, with at least two that make you stand out from other coaches in your organization/area.

- Write one or two paragraphs stating why someone should want to learn from you in a private lesson setting.

- Order a small set of business cards specifically to advertise that you offer private lessons.

- Watch a local match or tournament and challenge yourself to speak with at least one parent while you're there.

# CHAPTER 9: SETTING GROUND RULES

In a perfect world, we would easily find players who want lessons. They would schedule a time with us to take a lesson. Then they would come in, learn, pay, and set up another lesson before leaving.

Unfortunately, it will rarely go this smoothly. No-shows, heavy traffic, bad weather, and forgotten wallets happen.

Trust me; I know it can feel uncomfortable to bring these things up before you start giving lessons to someone. But here's the thing: If you don't let athletes and their parents know some basic boundaries, you're going to get burned. Maybe not intentionally... but losing time and money is very likely if you don't have any rules in place.

There have been days where I drove 45-minutes to a facility, only to lose money on my court rental due to a last-minute cancellation.

The worst part? The same thing happened to me the following week, too. Instead of just telling you that you need to have lesson policies, I put together a list of rules I have for lessons that I now send to every family I work with.

Feel free to use them and adapt them to your needs, but this should get you through some of the more common situations you'll face!

*Once a private lesson has been confirmed, the following rules apply:*

- *A $25 fee will be due if the lesson is cancelled for any reason once the court space is reserved.*

- *The lesson will end promptly at the agreed-upon time. If your child is late to the court, we cannot extend the time for the lesson.*

- *Parents, siblings, and friends are welcome to attend the lesson and watch from the sideline. Additional players receiving instruction on the court means an additional charge.*

- *Payment is due at the end of every lesson. Cash, check, and Venmo are accepted.*

- *Please note that I do not offer discounts and will decline all requests received.*

You may think these rules are a little overboard or go without saying... but they're there for a reason!

The benefit of having these rules is that it makes it much more comfortable for you to enforce rules once they are broken or if boundaries are being pushed.

For example, that lesson that was cancelled last-minute where I lost money? My cancellation fee would have covered it if I had made sure to communicate my policies ahead of time.

You may be okay with discounts (many coaches are), and you may not want to include my fifth rule in your policies. However, I include this upfront because I do not want to get taken advantage of, and I am personally a horrible negotiator. By declining discounts ahead of time, I save myself the inevitable price reduction after even the slightest push-back on the cost of a lesson.

Furthermore, I set my price based on several factors and therefore feel that my prices are always fair. If you take the time to set your prices appropriately, there should be no reason you have to offer a discount if you don't want to.

## COMMUNICATING EXPECTATIONS

As I mentioned before, having policies is vital. But ensuring that you communicate these ahead of time is critical to your success! In addition to policies, you may also want to clarify what parents and players can expect when they come to a lesson.

I highly encourage you to draft an email that you share with everyone after agreeing to a lesson, but before scheduling your court time. This email should include your personal policies (as discussed in the previous section), and you should aim to answer some of the more frequently asked questions that players and their families have. This should be in writing, so they can access this information when it works best for them. An email is easy to refer to and allows for more information than a short text.

By creating an outline of what a private lesson entails, you will cut down on back and forth emails or phone calls. You will give families more confidence in your professionalism and set expectations appropriately. You can help them realize that lessons aren't a one-and-done solution for most issues and that players will be receiving much more feedback than they typically do.

After including your policies/rules in your email, I encourage you to explain your process of running lessons and your own expectations. An example of this section might look like this:

*Hi (insert parent name here),*

*I'm so excited to work with (player name)! To help you prepare for our first lesson, I wanted to share what a typical lesson looks like and some policies I have.*

*A Typical Lesson:*

- *Players should bring a full water bottle and use the restroom before the lesson begins.*

- *Players should arrive at the court about 5-minutes early to get their volleyball shoes and kneepads on.*

- *We will start with 2-3 minutes of light warm-ups before beginning skill work.*

- *We will work on the skills and techniques discussed ahead of time in 10-15-minute time frames.*

- *Players are encouraged to ask questions and ask for clarification at all times during the lesson.*

- *Drills to work on at home will be given if possible.*

You can include your policies and ground rules after you describe a typical lesson.

Although it may seem like overkill to go into so much detail, laying out exactly what players and parents can expect in lessons helps them feel less apprehensive when they walk into the gym for the first time. Especially with younger players who may have never taken a lesson before, the extra effort you put into sharing this basic information will help your lesson run smoothly.

Plus, after you write it down once, it's a simple "copy and paste" for every lesson after!

# RESULTS ARE NEVER PROMISED

Parents approach coaches for lessons because they think some extra time on the court will help their child. But when they talk to you, and before they schedule anything, many of them will want a fair amount of reassurance that lessons are a good idea. In fact, some parents will ask for a guarantee of results!

If you give in and offer guarantees, you're setting yourself up for failure. The success of the lesson largely falls on the shoulders of the athlete. Even the most competent, experienced coaches cannot take a player from sub to starter without tremendous effort by the athlete. And if the athlete doesn't entirely buy-in to the process? Forget it; their results will likely not be what the parents hoped for.

The player will get out of the lesson what they put in, and the goal of these lessons is an improvement in skill and knowledge, not a new or improved role on a team. You don't have control over the other players on their team, how another coach makes playing time decisions, or even who a coach chooses for their team in the first place. That being said, it would be almost impossible not to see some improvement (both mentally and skills-wise) after a few lessons.

You cannot guarantee outcomes, but you can assure

players and parents that you will give the athlete the opportunity to improve over time based on their own effort and dedication during the lesson. That's all you can do. The rest is up to them!

# CHAPTER 9 TO-DO LIST:

- Draft out your own policies and expectations email. Let it sit for a day or two and revisit your list. Is there anything you need to add? Clarify? Remove?

- Do your best to keep this short and sweet. Bullet points are ideal, and I suggest you remove as many extra words as possible. Parents skim emails, so it's best to eliminate the fluff!

- If something is particularly important, be sure to write it first and consider putting it in bold to capture the reader's attention.

# CHAPTER 10: THREE TYPES OF PLAYERS

Over the years, I've concluded that there are three main types of volleyball players. Frequently, frustration can build when you're unsure how to connect with an athlete. However, once you understand how to coach each type, I believe you will end more lessons feeling good about your work.

## THREE TYPES OF VOLLEYBALL PLAYERS:

- Players who love volleyball and want to learn and get better.

- Players who just want to have fun.

- Players who are there because their mom (or some other family member) signed them up.

We're going to go more in-depth on how to work with each type of player, but you'll probably be able to identify what type of player you're working with in the first 5-10 minutes of your lesson (even if you haven't worked with them before).

Let me be clear: Skill level plays a very small role in how you'll approach coaching these different players. Sure, the intensity will differ! But the structure, pace, and goals within the lesson will be different based on their personality.

I'm going to explain how to identify each type of player and how to coach them for the best lesson outcome. We'll also break down what a successful lesson looks like for each type of player.

## PLAYERS WHO WANT TO LEARN AND GET BETTER

How To Identify Them:

This type of player…

- Can focus on you when you're talking.

- Is ready on time.

- Is often older (think 14u and up), or they seem mature for their age.

- Responds directly to feedback.

- Asks questions.

- Is sometimes hesitant to ask for water or a break.

How To Coach Them:

- PUSH THEM. Start with fundamentals but rapidly work into more complicated skills and strategies if they're ready for it.

- Use a mixture of progressions with high intensity/high repetition drills.

- Use drills that are tiring and have a lot of movement. This player will not be satisfied with the lesson unless they go home tired and feel like they learned at least 1-2 new concepts.

- Focus your lesson on skill development and knowledge expansion.

- Point out when skills are performed correctly, specifically saying what was done well. They want concrete feedback. Think, "you did a great job of staying low as you moved to that ball" instead of "nice pass."

Not that you don't have to bring your "A" game to lessons with the other types of players, but with this athlete... you need to come prepared!

Success With This Athlete:

- Sweating and being pushed at the edge of their skill level.

- Reaching "milestones" to show that they are

improving.

- Learning one or two new concepts or strategies they can use in their next team practice or match.

## PLAYERS WHO WANT TO HAVE FUN

How To Identify Them:

This type of player…

- Can only pay attention for short amounts of time.

- May interrupt to share something funny.

- Looks away and starts to get "antsy" if you take too long to explain something.

- Is typically younger (think 13u and below).

- Quickly gets bored with basic drills.

- Shows emotion more than others.

- Clearly looks bored or laughs loudly, depending on how engaged they are in the drill.

How To Coach Them:

- Use drills that have rewards and accomplishments. Use a lot of games.

- Give them a goal to help them focus.

- If you are just doing reps with no real reward, they will get lazy and start looking at other courts, yawning, etc.

- Teach a skill for 3-5 minutes, get the basics out of the way, and then have games with progressions. For example: Teach setting form for three minutes. Once they have that down, transition into setting to target at middle. Then to outside. Then to back.

- Teach form, but instruct in more general terms. They tend to get bored with too many details.

- If possible, have games incorporate a focus on proper form.

- If they are laughing, stick with your drill a little longer. However, be sure to move on before it gets boring!

- Occasionally you can ask them what games or drills they want to play. Ask them what their favorite part of the lesson was, then plan more like that.

You're still teaching the sport and pushing the athlete, but you're catering your instruction to help them focus. As soon as they stop having fun, the lessons will stop being beneficial!

Success With This Athlete:

- Laughter throughout the lesson.

- A story for them to share with their family about a goal they accomplished.

- Moving quickly through skills at their pace. Not the slow pace they're used to at team practices and clinics where they get bored.

# PLAYERS WHO ARE THERE BECAUSE THEIR MOM SIGNED THEM UP

It pains me to say it, but not everybody loves volleyball.

And although I half-jokingly refer to this type of player as someone who is only there "because their mom signed them up," there is usually some truth to that statement. In most cases, the parent is often more excited for the lesson than the child.

I've broken this type into two sub-types to address subtle differences you may see in this kind of player. Still, the pace of instruction and how you approach these lessons will largely be the same.

These players are usually new to the sport (or sports in general) and may or may not be athletic. On occasion, you'll also get extremely talented athletes who are being pushed by their parents to succeed (more on parents later) and the player honestly just wants a break.

These will most likely be your most challenging sessions.

# WHEN A PLAYER IS NOT NATURALLY ATHLETIC OR IS NEW TO SPORTS

How To Identify Them:

This type of player…

- Is usually shy and avoids eye contact.

- Looks at their parents frequently if they're in the gym watching.

- Responds to you with short answers (or even no answer) to your questions.

- Typically walks everywhere, even after you tell them to hustle.

How To Coach Them:

Our ultimate goal with this type of player is to give them a positive experience with volleyball. I want you to pause for a second and put yourself in the shoes of a child who is at a lesson when they don't want to be.

I want you to think of at least three things this player wants to have happen as a result of the lesson they're taking with you.

Here are the top five things I would put on that list:

- They don't want to look stupid.

- They want it to end quickly.

- They want their parent/guardian to be happy at the end of the lesson.

- They want to be told "nice job."

- They want to feel confident.

Your list may or may not match mine, but the sentiment is likely the same. With that in mind, let's address a few ways to approach this lesson to make it as enjoyable as possible.

First, avoid saying things like, "okay, we're going to do something really *easy* next." If they can't do it, it will make them (and you!) feel horrible.

While we usually want our lessons to be fast-paced, it's okay to slow these lessons down! You'll get a feel for your particular player, but in general, I've found that talking them through things ahead of time and demonstrating even simple movements will help.

Doing things "together" can work too. For example, new players *despise* having you stand there and watch their first attempts at pretty much anything.

I've found that, if you can, going through the skill *with* them takes the pressure off of them. When I do this with my players, I don't even look at them! I just do the skill and ask them to follow along with me, while giving basic verbal cues of what I'm doing. This gives them the freedom to try something without fear of judgment.

You could do this when practicing footwork for setting, hitting, or passing. You can even serve simultaneously! Don't try to impress this player with your skill. They will feel dumb!

The name of the game here is patience.

I always encourage these players to let me know if there's something they really like as we're going through it. Then we can focus on that skill more. If it's clear that they're not having fun or success, move on or change tactics.

Success With This Athlete:

- Finding a skill they can perform with consistent results.

- Simple homework so they can practice the skill they enjoyed the most.

- Focusing on the enjoyment of the sport

throughout the lesson. Reminding this athlete about upcoming tryouts or talking about being on a team before they're ready can scare them away.

• Giving their family concrete examples of what the player did well so they can talk about the athlete's successes after the lesson.

• Potentially scheduling a group lesson with a friend who wants to learn volleyball. This lets your athlete show off their new skills and knowledge and bond with a buddy.

# WHEN A PLAYER IS BORDERLINE BURNT OUT

If you have a highly skilled player who is close to being burnt out, take some time at the beginning of your lesson to chat with them. You'll want to discuss how things are going and see if there's anything they want to focus on.

This is challenging because they have likely been trained to push through their lack of motivation. You may get fake answers as opposed to real responses! These players will usually have one or two things that they say they want to work on. Most of the time, these are things the parents told them they need to work on (as opposed to genuinely wanting to get better themselves).

Have some sympathy for these players if things aren't going well. Patience will go a long way. They're going to need to trust that you want what's best for them and that you care about them before they start to perform!

You will need a higher level of technical knowledge for this lesson, so get as much info ahead of time about what they want to work on. This way, you can brush up on your skills beforehand and come packed with knowledge and explanations to walk them through challenges.

Essentially, you need to break up their limiting beliefs about themselves to push through and make progress. Don't promise you will be able to fix something, because if your first strategy or technique doesn't work for that player, you lose them.

How To Identify Them:

This type of player…

- Listens closely, but seems less enthusiastic about the lesson.

- Typically jogs everywhere. They've been trained to hustle, but they do it out of habit rather than a desire to move quickly.

- Gets frustrated easily with repeat failures but seems more sad than mad.

- Seems like they're holding back information in conversation. Like they don't want to say how they actually feel.

## How To Coach This Player:

For this lesson:

- Consult with the player for 2-3 minutes in the beginning (away from their parent) so you can have an honest conversation about what they need or want to work on. Feel free to ask about parent and coach expectations to learn more about what is holding them back. You're not there to disagree with their parent or coach, but sometimes players are held back by the things they feel they can't say aloud, like "I don't want to play middle anymore." This can be tricky to navigate, but always encourage the player while supporting their parent or coach.

- Start slow with some warm-ups for the skill in question and then move into trouble-shooting mode. They will likely point out when they mess up. Watch them a few times to really assess their weaknesses, and then start trying solutions. For example, their hit is always going out of bounds. A possible solution could be to shorten the approach to keep the ball in front of them as they make contact. They might also try to follow through fully to get more topspin on the ball, swing their arms up faster to get a little extra height on the jump, or swing softer and work on placement, etc.

- Found a solution? Great! Reinforce how to fix it and then move on to the next issue.

<u>Success With This Athlete:</u>

- Identify at least one solution to a major barrier they're facing.

- Consistent successful repetitions of a skill at the edge of their ability.

- Have them leave with more confidence after the lesson, which often looks like a smile and a sense of relief for this player.

# CHAPTER 11: INTERACTING WITH PARENTS

Keep in mind that not everyone who signs a child up for lessons is the parent of that child. It may be a grandparent, aunt, mom's boyfriend, cousin, guardian… remember that when communicating with the family. For simplicity, I refer to the person who brings the player to your lesson as the parent.

That being said, when you're communicating with parents, there are three broad experiences you're sure to face. Although there are plenty of different personality types, I've found there are only a few themes that really emerge when interacting with parents. And those are:

- Mainly positive interactions

- Mainly neutral interactions

- Mainly negative interactions

While these classifications aren't exactly "earth-shattering," I've seen too many coaches approach all parents in the same manner. By being aware of the tone of the interactions you're having with parents, you can adjust your communication style to have a more positive experience overall.

You probably expect parents to be enthusiastic about their child's lessons... I know I do! But as it turns out, that's not always the case. Whether that's due to a busy work schedule, a personal lack of interest in sport, or just a hectic time in their life, not all parents will be excited to discuss the progress their athlete is making.

In fact, some parents can even come off as abrasive in certain circumstances! But once you understand how to communicate in these different situations, you'll make your relationship with them much more enjoyable.

## MAINLY POSITIVE INTERACTIONS

I doubt I need to say it, but I'm going to say it anyway... When you have primarily positive interactions with parents, your job is a *lot* easier!

They may or may not have volleyball experience, but they love that their child enjoys lessons with you, and that is what's important to them. Often very friendly, they'll normally walk into the gym smiling and give you an update on how their child has been doing since your last lesson.

Positive parents may or may not be able to stay and watch the lesson, but if they do, you'll probably hear "good job!" or "way to go!" frequently from the sideline.

Tips For Working With Positive Parents:

- Keep interactions short; don't get caught up in conversation and start your lesson late.

- Don't overpromise. With a willing audience, it's hard to refrain from talking about all the incredible things that can come out of lessons!

- Say thank you. Happy, positive parents will often give you compliments. Instead of shrugging them off, just say that you appreciate the kind words and mentally store their feedback for a rainy day.

- Don't offer extras just because they're nice. Discounted lessons, longer lessons... you might feel that you need to offer something in return for kind words. They might even ask for these things, and you'll probably feel guilted into a "yes." It's okay to say "no" and to continue operating as planned!

- Enjoy your conversations, but keep things professional. Even if a parent is kind to you, as you get to know them, they may not turn out to be as friendly as you initially thought. If you start to loosen up after a few lessons and mention that another coach does something "wrong" or "doesn't know what they're doing," it can come back to haunt you later.

Overall, working with positive parents will typically result in an enjoyable lesson. In my own experience, you'll work with parents who are mainly positive about 50% of the time.

## MAINLY NEUTRAL INTERACTIONS

Sometimes, it can be tough to read a parent, especially if they only have time to drop off and pick up their child. Parents who interact with you in a mainly neutral way don't necessarily give you tons of praise for the work you're doing, but they don't complain, either.

Many of these parents either don't have much to say, or their lives are just busy. While the positive parent may leave you feeling like you are a great coach, a parent who gives little to no feedback can make you question if they're satisfied with the lessons.

Having worked with quite a few parents who fall into this category and having overanalyzed their reactions to the lessons I gave their kids, I realized a few things to keep in mind when interacting with this type of parent.

Tips For Working With Neutral Parents:

- They probably want conversations with you to be short and sweet. Summarize the highlights from your lesson quickly and succinctly so they can get out of the gym.

- Don't overanalyze. Having done this myself, I've learned to accept that some families just aren't as interested in their child's private lessons as you might expect!

- Quiet or neutral reactions don't necessarily mean dissatisfaction.

- These parents are often very busy and don't have time to chat.

- Communicate more with the player about their progress and how they can continue to improve. Lesson recaps will be discussed towards the end of the book, but with neutral parents, it is probably the player who is pushing for lessons. Focus on giving them the information you'd normally give to parents.

The greatest difficulty with neutral parents is that they can be hard to read. My best suggestion? Just continue to assume everything is going well unless they say otherwise. You can check-in with them every once in a while to make sure they're happy, but don't overdo it.

In my own coaching experience, about 30% of parents I've worked with have tended to be more neutral in our interactions.

## MAINLY NEGATIVE INTERACTIONS

You'd think that parents who seek you out to work with their child would be happy about the lessons, right?

Well… for the most part, that's true! If parents arrange lessons and continue to come back, they're happy with the lessons for one reason or another. The problem is, sometimes they don't always show it.

Negative parents can be a little tricky to work with, but once you've learned how to identify them and manage their negativity, you can still build a good relationship with them!

Negative interactions don't necessarily mean the parent is a bad person. But if you're not ready to deal with the negativity, it can wear you out! A few examples of negative interactions include parents who:

- Repeatedly complain about the high cost of lessons and always ask for a discount.

- Are unhappy with other coaches in their child's life.

- Don't think their child is progressing fast enough to keep up with others in the same grade.

Honestly, these are the same concerns that most parents have! It's just that these individuals tend to verbalize their feelings more harshly. And if you're sensitive like me, it can be tough to learn to communicate with someone who has more negative things to say than positive. Here are the ways I've learned to interact with negative parents while keeping things professional.

Tips For Working With Negative Parents:

- Listen. Often people complain over and over about something because they feel like they're not being heard! If parents continue to bring up something negative, they might just need someone to acknowledge their complaints.

- Ask questions. If a parent is complaining about something, by asking a few questions you can get to the bottom of the issue and move on. Do they keep complaining about their kid's high school coach? After a couple of questions, maybe you uncover that the parent doesn't understand how rotations work. What an excellent opportunity to educate and improve their experience!

- Stick to your beliefs. Sometimes I flat out refuse to teach kids certain concepts when I believe it won't be beneficial. I've then had parents find another coach who would teach those things and then come back to tell me I was wrong, more or less. And? I encourage them to continue lessons with that coach if that is what's working best for them. I'm not about to go against my coaching philosophy just for a couple of extra bucks.

- It's probably not you. Maybe they just got laid off. Maybe a family member is sick. Maybe they are in the middle of buying a house, and the stress is really getting to them. Who knows what is going on outside of the gym. The best thing you can do is just continue to be a positive coach for their child and make sure the negativity doesn't impact you.

- Avoid being wishy-washy. Perhaps the family keeps asking for a discount and complains that your prices are too high. Maybe they complain that the gym you give lessons out of is too far away and want you to drive out to them. If you have no interest in changing your prices or location, just say "no." And say it firmly! You can set expectations early by setting rules, but if people start to try to push you around, just say "no" and remind them of your rules.

- Refuse to be negative. It's easy to dismiss negative chatter when you disagree with what someone is saying. But what about it if you agree with them? What if you think that their daughter's 8th-grade coach, for example, really *doesn't* know what they are doing? It can be tempting to finally agree on something and build rapport around any topic, even if it is negative. But don't. That's a road you don't want to go down.

When you tend to have more negative interactions with someone, rather than positive ones, lessons become unappealing and start to wear on you. Although I don't frequently come across negative parents (only about 20% of the time), they can drag you down if you let them.

While using these tips might help you keep your interactions polite and allow you to work with players you otherwise enjoy, you don't necessarily have to continue working with them. But we'll get into that towards the end of the book.

# CHAPTER 12: SIX TYPES OF LESSONS

Sometimes it isn't enough to just say that you offer private lessons. I like to categorize my lessons based on different needs that players and parents have, making it easier for them to say "yes" to lessons. Because honestly, "private lessons" just sounds... expensive.

But we can give them a better idea of what they will get out of the lesson so they'll be more interested in learning more, without saying "no" right away. I've included a list of six types of lessons you can offer to better convey what you'll be teaching your athletes.

## 1. ALL SKILLS

<u>What It Is:</u>

A quick review of the basics (passing, setting, hitting, and serving). These players don't always have a specific position or skill they want to practice, but they are looking to gain confidence across the board.

## Who To Advertise To:

Young athletes, in particular, are more likely to get signed up for this type of lesson because they're not on a team yet and are not in-season.

7th through 9th-grade players will be interested in this type of lesson when they're getting ready for tryouts (of course, only a week before), and they want a couple of lessons to get their general skill level up quickly. Keep this time open on your calendar to maximize the number of lessons you can give!

## When To Advertise:

- Year-round for athletes in 6th grade and below.
- Right before tryout time for middle school and high school students. These are popular for incoming 6th/7th and 9th-grade students who are starting at a new school with a new program.

# 2. SKILLS EVALUATION

<u>What It Is:</u>

A review of the basics, possibly including an assessment by you for position guidance. Typically, you'll only run this type of lesson once with each player you work with.

You'll want to get some background information before you run this one. It's essential to know things like what position(s) they have played before, do their teammates play for prominent club programs, their main coach's background, etc. After one Skills Evaluation lesson, you'll usually move on to lesson types three or four listed later in this section.

<u>When To Advertise:</u>

Primarily in the weeks leading up to tryouts. Summer, in general, is a popular time for this type of lesson.

<u>Who To Advertise To:</u>

Again, players entering a new school or a new program (7th grade, 9th grade) will want to take lessons and get feedback on what the player does well, and they will want to know position ideas from a coach.

You can't guarantee that future coaches will agree with your assessment, but for the most part, you can place someone into front-row, back-row, or as a setter. This depends on a variety of factors, such as the performance of each skill, height, and volleyball IQ.

*There are rules regarding evaluations for schools and clubs. Be sure to check the regulations of your governing body before "evaluating" anyone.

# 3. SPECIFIC SKILL WORK

<u>What It Is:</u>

When a player wants to get better at a specific skill in particular. These often fall into the basic categories of passing, setting, hitting, and serving, but in my experience, I get a lot of lessons for serving only.

If you played in college or are particularly good at a certain skill, you can also brand yourself as a "setting coach" or "hitting coach." Although this could take away some lessons (defensive specialists might look elsewhere), if demand is high in your area, you might benefit more from branding yourself this way.

<u>When To Advertise:</u>

Before tryouts and early in the season when players

realize they are behind in a skill after a couple of team practices.

Who To Advertise To:

Any age you feel comfortable working with. Ideally, players will be on an organized team of some sort that has competitions. Players below 7th grade likely won't be interested in this type of lesson unless it is a serving lesson. I suggest offering All Skills lessons (instead of Specific Skill Work lessons) to players in 6th grade and below unless you are in a highly competitive area.

# 4. POSITION TRAINING

What It Is:

Position training is when players know what position they're playing or have a goal position they're trying out for. You'll run lessons based more on situational learning rather than fundamental skill development.

Here are a few examples of position training. Middle blocker lessons: work on attack placement, blocking footwork, overhead passing. Libero training: *lots* of passing work, but also training for serving, hitting back-row attacks, and training for "setter-out" situations. For setter training, think jump sets, one-handed sets, tempo work, defense, serving, etc.

When To Advertise:

Before tryouts (always popular) and throughout the playing season. Club players are more likely to have time for this type of lesson (school has practice or competitions every weekday), but you may get in some weekend sessions during the school season if availability allows.

Who To Advertise To:

7th grade and up, *or* players who have gone through your skill evaluation lesson *and* you feel confident you can start training them in a position. My advice? Don't lock a 6th-grader into setter training unless you can see without a doubt that she'll excel in this area. Continue to keep her well-rounded just in case other coaches evaluate her skillset differently.

# 5. CUSTOMIZED LONG-TERM PLAN

What It Is:

This type of lesson can be all over the place. You'll want to check in with players and parents frequently to make sure lessons are running as expected.

You don't want to lose a long-term lesson because you started focusing too much on skills training when they were expecting you to evaluate and train based on a position. Always come prepared with a few directions in mind, and leave the final decision to the player/parent.

For example, after we greet each other, I'll say something along the lines of, "Hey Julie, I thought you did a good job of setting the last time we saw each other. I have a really fun lesson planned if you want to keep working on your setting skills, or we could work on your hitting and blocking today. What do you think?"

If you get a long pause, you can also ask if there's something else they want to work on. If you *still* get no response or they don't have a preference, just go with whatever you think will be the most fun and beneficial for the player.

Keep in mind: it's easy to get burnt out with volleyball lessons as a player. If you start to see less enthusiasm, you better step it up! Otherwise, you're going to lose the lesson soon!

When To Advertise:

You can advertise this type of lesson throughout the year, but summer will probably be the most popular time for many families.

Many players will often sign up for lessons with some sort of an end goal in mind, so you'll probably work with them for up to two months before they get what they want out of the arrangement.

However, with long-term plans, parents may just be looking for a way to get their child moving, start their kids in sports before they're old enough to play on a team, or lessons might even be a fun alternative to babysitting. For these reasons, you should offer these types of lessons throughout the year.

Who To Advertise To:

Younger players just starting, or older players with some sort of a goal in mind will often be the players you get for long-term lessons.

The 5th and 6th graders who have an extra hour after school before mom and dad can pick them up, or the high school junior focused on playing in college are both just as likely to ask for long-term plans.

# 6. GROUP LESSONS

What It Is:

Group lessons are when you have two or more athletes attend a single session. Although coaches can offer group lessons with as many players as they want, the typical number of participants is two. When you start to include more people, your ability to work individually with each player shrinks. As such, the price per person drops. Pricing your group lessons is discussed in chapter 18, so we'll go into more detail there.

Group lessons can fall into any of the previous categories discussed in this chapter. Typically, this is based on the time of year and age of the participants. The structure of group lessons is discussed in-depth in chapter 18, so all you need to know for now is that a group lesson is when you're juggling focus between two or more players.

When To Advertise:

You can advertise group lessons at any time. I've found these are particularly popular during the summer when parents are looking for activities for their children, and about a month after seasons start. This happens because players are on teams, have made friends, and now want to improve together.

Who To Advertise To:

Let everyone know when you're advertising lessons that you offer group lessons as well. You will likely be asked about group lessons after one or two successful lessons with individual players. When athletes have a positive experience with you and start telling their friends, other players and their families become interested!

The reduction in price per athlete is also a little easier for most families, and since the benefit of lessons can still be just as high in a group setting, this may be the preferred method for some families.

# CHAPTER 13: PLANNING YOUR LESSON

Coaches, I want you to know that scheduling and running private lessons takes a lot of work upfront. At this point, you're probably wondering when we're going to talk about giving the lesson! And we're *basically* there. We're to the point now where we're going to plan out your first lesson, and it's imperative that you spend time on this step. Honestly, this is probably the most important part of the whole lesson process!

Planning a great lesson will come naturally after a few sessions. Even though you may feel like you sink a lot of time into the first five or six lessons you run, know that it will get easier!

I don't want to put *too* much pressure on you, but if you run a great lesson, you're going to have a much easier time getting your next one! That is why it is so critical to spend some time on this step.

While your lesson's content will vary widely based on the player(s) you're working with, there are a few general concepts to keep in mind.

## PLANNING YOUR LESSON

**Step 1**: *Always* print or write down your lesson. No phones out, ever. As I mentioned in the chapter on equipment, if you want to use video, bring a tablet specifically for volleyball use. I'll include an outline that I use when I'm drafting my own lessons at the end of this chapter, so you can use that to get started.

**Step 2**: Think about *pace*. Some skills are a little slower than others, and sometimes you need to pause the action to talk. But an hour will go by *very* quickly, and you're going to have a lot to get through. You need to minimize breaks and reduce general slowness. Additionally, if there's a lot of standing around, your chance of getting a repeat lesson drops pretty quickly. Parents won't see much value if all you're doing is standing around talking.

**Step 3**: *Minimize* shagging and *maximize* touches on the ball. When planning drills to run, keep in mind that you probably only have 10-15 balls in your ball cart. You'll want to run drills that don't require shagging every 2-minutes.

You can also ask parents and siblings to shag for you

(if the facility allows them on the court, check first). Just be sure to give them instructions on *how* to shag. Otherwise, they'll likely make the rookie mistake of rolling the ball back to where you're standing and possibly injure their own player.

Group Lessons Note: I highly recommend having at least two ball carts if you have more than two players. I made this mistake once and felt like I wasted a lot of time making the girls shag after three or four contacts on the ball each.

**Step 4**: Save the best drill for last. What I mean by that is to save the drill that will "show off" what the player learned for the end of the lesson. This is usually when the parents come back to the court (if they left), and you want to demonstrate the value that a private lesson gives. Personally, I like to bust out targets of some sort or run a very high-tempo drill.

**Step 5**: Set up beforehand. Don't wait until your lesson shows up to drag the boxes out or to run and grab a ball cart. Starting late makes you look unprofessional.

If it makes sense, run your most "equipment heavy" drills first so you can set up equipment before your time starts. Or give the player a water break and hustle to get things set up. Parents *really* appreciate coaches who move quickly, because they feel like they're getting their money's worth. This is *especially* true if they've taken lessons with someone else before and had a bad experience.

That being said, make sure you don't jump into a skill just because you require a lot of equipment! If you want to use boxes to work on arm swing, for example, you probably don't want to start the lesson with this because your athlete's arm will take a bit to get warmed up. Having boxes ready to go on the side will make this transition much faster and show that you planned well ahead of time.

**Step 6**: This might be controversial, but... you're entertaining as much as you are teaching. I realized this about a year into giving lessons. Keeping that in mind, I increased the number of lessons I was giving and the overall satisfaction from families. You want happy players and happy parents; you're not there to run the kids into the ground! Make sure you're *teaching*, and that every drill is much more skills-focused rather than entertainment-focused... but let's face it. Your lessons need to be fun!

Now that you've got a general idea of how to plan your lesson, I want to share a sample lesson plan with you. This is a plan I've used with multiple ages at varying skill levels.

# SAMPLE LESSON PLAN: LIBERO OR DEFENSIVE SPECIALIST

**5-minutes**: Run two laps, stretches, 15 service tosses, 15 wall traps, and "Serve-To-Me Progressions" (drill #1 in the back of this book).

**10-minutes**: Serve anywhere with zones marked, form review, and accuracy work if the player is ready for it (drill #3).

**10-minutes**: Passing to target from a toss over the net (free ball passing form), moving side to side, moving from deep to short, and vice versa.

**10-minutes**: Passing to target from coach's hit from a box from outside, middle, and right side. Player can start in their defensive position or work on transition from base to defense, depending on skill level (drill #4).

**10-minutes**: Serve-receive pass to target, move to cover hitters (outside, middle, or right side) and pass high "blocked" ball. (Coach will serve and then run to a ball cart at the net to toss a second ball over, mimicking a blocked attack).

**10-minutes**: Down ball and back-row attack review, setup targets in deep corners if player is ready to work on aim (drill #8).

**5-minutes**: Serve and move to base, transition into defense and pass to target from coach's hit off box (or free ball toss, depending on age and skill level).

**Wrap-Up**: Discuss their strengths, areas for improvement, and how to practice at home.

Although I have "5-minutes" or "10-minutes" written in my plans, these are all pretty fluid. It is very likely I would make changes to my plan as I progressed through the lesson. In fact, sticking precisely to this schedule as it is written would likely result in a less-than-ideal lesson because it is so full.

So... why write the plan like this? *It gives me options.*

Let's say that as the lesson progresses and we get to our third drill on the list (passing to a target from a free ball), our player starts to struggle. In this example, maybe it's particularly true for when they are working on moving from "short" to "deep" to pass.

There are a couple of things you can do because of the way you've structured your plan.

You can either, A) cut the drill short and move on, leaving out short to deep movements for the day, or B) spend a little more time on this area if the player is close to getting it.

With a schedule that is so full, you can easily cut

something out to allow for more time on the basics or cut something short because you have enough planned to fill an entire hour anyway. If you cut it short, notice how the 5-minute drill scheduled for the end of the hour can easily become a 10-minute drill (or even a 15-minute drill, since it works on all of the skills covered that day).

I personally like to ask players, "do you want to stick with this until you get it, or do you want to move on?"

Of course, you can decide for them. But when I'm working with a new player and don't fully understand their reactions to failures or frustrations, asking them their preference helps me learn how to proceed in the future when they face another challenge.

Note: this doesn't mean we won't work on the skill ever again! Maybe it's just better left for another day, or even later in the lesson if time permits.

Using my template as an example, try to create your own lesson plan. I've given you prompts, but it's up to you to decide how you want to spend the time.

Not sure where to start? Try creating a lesson plan for the age you primarily coach for a setter (or a player who is naturally good at setting if they are too young to have positions yet) and who also wants to work on their serve.

# LESSON PLAN TEMPLATE

| | |
|---|---|
| __:__ - __:__ | Quick full-body warm-up and skill-specific warm-up. |
| __:__ - __:__ | Skill-specific drill focusing on 1-2 techniques. |
| __:__ - __:__ | Second skill-specific drill starting with first progression. |
| __:__ - __:__ | Second skill-specific drill moving to second progression. |
| __:__ - __:__ | Situational drill using previous skill(s). |
| __:__ - __:__ | Minor skill work - fast moving and high-rep. |
| __:__ - __:__ | Game-like drill combining most or all skills. |

# CHAPTER 13 TO-DO LIST:

Design a lesson plan using the provided outline based on a player you think you might be able to get a lesson with.

Feeling good about the lesson you designed? Great! Challenge yourself to create a lesson for these scenarios as well:

- An 8th grader who is hoping to make the "A" team at their middle school. They don't have a position yet, but they are tall. Plan a lesson to test most skills (Evaluation Lesson) with a focus on front-row skill development at the end (assuming this is where most middle school coaches will place a taller player).

- A high school freshman has just made the 16u team at the local club. She has never set before, but the coach is using her in this position. Create a lesson to assess her current skill at setting and then build on her strengths and improve areas of weakness.

- The local rec program is growing, and the mother of a 10-year-old has reached out because her daughter absolutely loves volleyball but struggles with her overhand serve. Draft a lesson plan that will focus on her serve, and think of a few backup drills in case her arm needs a rest or if she gets frustrated.

# CHAPTER 14: RUNNING YOUR LESSON

When it comes to running a lesson, especially the first few times, it's easy to feel overwhelmed by the pressure to perform. When I first started giving lessons, I felt very anxious every time I'd step on the court. I would constantly keep an eye on the clock, overanalyze every facial expression my athlete made, and in general, I was just stressed out!

I wanted to do a good job, but without a real understanding of how to coach a private lesson or what was expected of me, I made it a lot harder on myself than it needed to be!

Running a lesson is similar to coaching a team because you are teaching volleyball. However, I've learned that there are a few key differences between running a practice and running a lesson! In this chapter, I'll share some tips to help you run a great private lesson.

Keep in mind that each lesson is specific to the player and their goals. You'll likely change the intensity, pacing, and rhythm of the practice based on the type of player you're working with and the goals they have for the lesson. But there are a few principles that we can use throughout every lesson to make it more beneficial for our players.

**Limit corrections**. When we're coaching a team, we're often shouting out correction after correction, trying to help as many players as we possibly can. You may be used to constantly providing feedback while on the court, so staying silent for a rep or two might feel unnatural. In a lesson, however, it can be overwhelming for a single player to receive non-stop instruction!

While it can be tempting to suggest a small tweak to their footwork after one rep, and a change in upper body motion after the next, pick the change that will benefit them the most and allow them to focus on making that change for a few reps. My suggestion? I always start with the feet and footwork, since being in the right place (or not) usually has the biggest impact on their form. Once they're getting to the right spot in the right manner, we can progress to additional corrections.

**Be okay with slow progress**. It can be discouraging to watch a player struggle. Especially when they're enthusiastic about something and their parent is there watching, but no matter what tactic you try, something just isn't clicking.

For example, I ran *multiple* lessons with a relatively strong 13-year-old who struggled to get her serve over. And by struggled, I mean… she could not get a *single serve over*. Not one! After two one-hour lessons, she still had not gotten a serve over from behind the end line. Quite frankly, she even struggled to get the ball over the net from the middle of the court.

No matter what techniques we tried, the homework I gave her, the mental coaching I provided… nothing was working.

We only ended up doing two lessons together since the lessons were to prepare her for tryouts the following week. Personally, it was tremendously disheartening to spend so much effort trying to help her reach what I perceived to be a simple goal, and yet, she wasn't able to achieve it during our lessons.

After her tryouts, she was so excited to tell me that she had gotten a few serves over, and I was thrilled for her! But it can be tough as a coach not to see immediate results! Fortunately, this player and her mother were extremely excited that she eventually got a few serves over the net. Still, I imagine most parents in this situation might start to express concern or worry if their son or daughter hadn't gotten a single serve over after two lessons.

What I'm trying to explain here is, no matter how quickly you think a player *should* be able to progress, or how much they *want* to execute a skill, sometimes it just takes time! This is why I highly encourage coaches *not* to promise any outcomes as a result of lessons. The fact is, you just don't know how a player is going to advance. Setting expectations too high and then failing to meet them is a recipe for disaster and discouragement.

**Train more than just skills**. Learning how to hit down the line and cross-court is fun. But the real payoff is when a player knows *why* they might choose one over the other! When you're coaching one-on-one, it is a great time to offer in-depth explanations into why an athlete might make one choice over another. Of course, you're not pausing the lesson to give a 10-minute speech! But after a player starts to show that they can execute a more advanced skill, take a minute or two to explain game applications, different scenarios where the skill might come in handy, and how to make those decisions.

I especially like having this conversation in front of the parent if they're in attendance, or at least talking loud enough so they can hear! Based on my own experience as a player, I know that learning occurs on the court, but processing and talking everything through happens on the car ride home! If you can educate a parent or two along the way, you're going to have an even bigger impact on your volleyball community.

On the following page is another sample lesson plan. Note that I've included her age and goals. Think about potential *extras* that you might point out as you progress through the lesson.

Imagine the feedback you might give to her, visualizing yourself focusing on only one or two major corrections you might make. What strategic tips could you give her? Any fun side comments?

# SAMPLE VOLLEYBALL LESSON PLAN

Kelcie in 8th Grade, 6:00pm-7:00pm

Preparing for Tryouts | No Position | 1st of 4 weekly lessons

Goal of lesson: Identify areas of strength to develop and suggest possible positions.

6:00pm-6:15pm

- 2 warm-up laps
- Short arm warm-up progression
- Serve-To-Me serving progressions
  - Analyze form first, correct one to two major issues. Emphasize what she is doing well and her strengths.

6:15pm-6:25pm

- Ball control assessment
- Make minor corrections and determine passing strengths and weaknesses.
  - Passing from a free ball over the net directly to her.
  - Passing from a free ball over the net to the left.
  - Passing a free ball over the net to the

right.

    o   Passing a down ball over the net.

6:25pm-6:35pm

- Setting assessment

- Make minor corrections and determine setting strengths and weaknesses.

    o   Set to middle from a toss.

    o   Set to outside from a toss.

    o   Set to right side from a toss.

6:35pm-6:45pm

- Hitting assessment

- Make minor corrections and determine hitting strengths and weaknesses.

    o   Hit from middle from a toss.

    o   Hit from outside from a toss.

    o   Hit from right side from a toss.

    o   Hit a down ball from a toss.

6:45pm-7:00pm

- Spend 2-3 minutes discussing potential positions, strengths, weaknesses, and favorite skills (preferably during a water break). Run more advanced drills in areas of interest.

(Ex: Kelcie enjoyed setting and seems like a good fit for a setter, but also excelled in passing.)

- Set to targets starting in setter positions.

- Set to targets starting from right back transitioning to the setter position.

- Set to targets starting from setter position transitioning to the 10' line.

7:00pm-7:05pm

- Wrap-up with parent to discuss lesson highlights, ways to practice at home if desired, schedule the next lesson, and collect payment.

# CHAPTER 15: MAKING ADJUSTMENTS

No matter how much effort you put into planning your lesson, one thing is almost certain: you will need to make adjustments.

While you're running your lesson, it's likely that you won't stick to your plan 100%. Something on the schedule (for example, hitting to the deep corners) may be either *too* advanced or not advanced *enough*. In situations like these, you must make changes on the fly to keep the player pushing themselves. But make sure you write down your adjustments! This might be challenging at first, but will get easier with practice.

Why is it so important that you write down the changes you make? Well, it may be easy to remember how your lesson goes when you've only got one a week. But once you get to three a week or have been running lessons for a month or so, they'll all start to blend together. That's why you should track any adjustments made!

This way, the next time you're planning a lesson with this player, you will have a quick refresher and can build off of what you did (or didn't) do! I haven't *personally* done it, but I imagine it'd reflect poorly on you if you use the same drill twice with one player two weeks in a row without remembering or acknowledging it.

Besides adjusting for skill level, you might need to make changes because the player isn't feeling well, they come in and they have an injury, or your equipment gets lost/broken/isn't working anymore. Keep track of this as well, and follow up if necessary.

## CHOOSE DRILLS WITH FLEXIBILITY IN MIND

When it comes to choosing drills, I highly recommend using ones that allow a certain amount of versatility. Most drills can be adjusted, but I'll admit that there have been a few times I've been stumped about how to alter a drill! What ends up happening is that you completely abandon the skill or drill you had planned, and if you struggle to think on your feet or if you're new to lessons, you might waste a few minutes trying to come up with a different idea.

Spending even a couple of minutes trying to work out

a new drill, trying something new, and then switching again… this causes you to appear unprofessional. And it won't feel that great, either!

Luckily, if you know this ahead of time, you can avoid the trap of choosing drills with little to no wiggle room.

Fortunately, most drills are pretty flexible. All you need to think about is whether you want to make the drill more or less challenging, and then decide the change that best applies to the skill you're working on.

On the following page is a quick cheat-sheet for ways to make adjustments to almost any drill.

# HOW TO ALTER DRILLS

| Possible Changes | Make It Less Challenging | Make It More Challenging |
|---|---|---|
| Change the pace of the ball | Slower | Faster |
| Change the angle of the ball | Higher | Lower |
| Change the target area | Bigger | Smaller |
| Change the player's speed | Slower | Faster |
| Change the goal number | Less | More |
| Change the time spent on the skill | Slower (more time on drill) | Faster (less time on drill) |
| Change the complexity | Remove a step | Add a step |

Note: Depending on the situation, these suggestions could also be reversed.

# MAKE A DRILL LESS CHALLENGING

Let's say a 14u player is working on passing from left back. She is transitioning from base to her defensive positions, and you started the drill by hitting the ball to her. You've set up an empty cart in right front as her target.

After about five or six reps, the player hasn't made a pass anywhere close to the target. You watch a little more closely and realize she's practically tripping over herself trying to move into defense.

While we want to challenge our athletes, the current scenario is too difficult for her. If we continue to run the drill as-is, her confidence will likely drop, and she will not learn from the lesson or may not even enjoy it that much.

We need to make this drill easier for her! The following page features possible changes we could make to finish this drill on a good note.

| **Possible Changes** | **Make It Less Challenging** |
|---|---|
| Change the pace of the ball | Swing easier to give the player more time to transition. |
| Change the angle of the ball | Instead of hitting the ball, do a roll-shot to slow down the ball. |
| Change the target area | Lay out cones marking a wider area as her target, taking some pressure off of her. |
| Change the player's speed | Have the player transition first, and *then* you hit the ball. |
| Change the goal number | If your goal was to get 15 passes to target, stop counting until she gets a couple to target. Then do 3 more to finish the drill. |
| Change the time spent on the skill | Spend more time on this drill if it is important to them. If not, move on to another drill. |
| Change the complexity | Remove the transition and have them pass starting in defensive position. Add the footwork after they get their confidence back. |

As you can see, there are many ways to alter the most basic drills to make them less challenging. Since our player struggled with her footwork, changes regarding the speed of her transition will likely be the most beneficial. You can also make multiple changes if needed.

But what about when a drill is too *easy* for a player?

## MAKE A DRILL MORE CHALLENGING

Let's say you're working with a 16u player, and you're going to work on her serving. You've got cones laid out, marking the different zones and plan to improve her accuracy.

As soon as you start the drill, you realize that the player rarely misses the intended zone, and even if it's not the *right* zone, it's very close. On top of that, she's got good pace behind her serve, and her form is excellent.

Making a drill more challenging for an advanced player can seem overwhelming if you're not ready with options! Note that sometimes not *every* option is a great idea for the specific skill. And keep in mind that these are just *some* ideas. I'm sure you can come up with many more on your own!

| Possible Changes | Make It More Challenging |
|---|---|
| Change the pace of the ball | Try working on short serves. Versatility could make this player a more valuable server. |
| Change the angle of the ball | If the serve has an arc to it, attempt to make it flatter (below the top of the antennae). |
| Change the target area | Mark off areas of the court rather than zones (like seams). |
| Change the player's speed | If a player is already serving with good pace, don't try to add more. This could result in unnecessary fatigue or injury. |
| Change the goal number | If hitting every target is too easy, change it to hitting every target several times. |
| Change the time spent on the skill | It's okay to move on to other drills where you can give more value. |
| Change the complexity | Teach them to jump serve. |

Increasing the difficulty is usually more challenging than making a drill easier for a player, but it's definitely possible!

While there are a ton of options, you may switch up your approach based on your athlete. For example, maybe the player has no interest in learning how to jump serve, or they have a past injury that makes you hesitant to push them to serve harder or faster. Making their targets smaller or even moving on from this drill early makes more sense.

And in the case of our 14u passer, if she's taking lessons because she wants to play in the back-row for the top team at her school, we need to make sure she can transition. Slowing down the drill until she learns the footwork is important to her long-term success. Letting her get out of the drill early or moving on too quickly won't do her any favors.

Adjustments are critical to keeping the athlete mentally in the drill. Too few successes, and even too *many* successes, can lead to lower interest, less effort, and less growth.

# CHAPTER 16: LESSON REVIEW AND WRAP-UP

Alright! The hour is over and it's time to wrap-up your lesson. Instead of going to the parent with your hand out for the check, I like to approach the parent and call the player over for a recap. I have a usual "script" that I follow with almost every lesson. Having an outline in place helps me cover what is important. In this lesson recap, I like to cover the following topics:

- Point out at *least* one thing the player did really well and describe it in detail. I've given lessons to some very low-skilled players, and trust me. You can always find *something* to compliment them on. You can then add another one or two things they did with a high level of skill or enthusiasm.

- If your athlete struggled with a certain skill,

acknowledge it, but point out how they can overcome that challenge. Let them know it's something they *will* be able to work through with more practice. Did something go poorly? It's okay to suggest focusing on other skills if it was really that bad (remember: players do not have to excel at *every* skill).

- Keep it simple. If you're going to talk about topspin, float serves, down balls, free balls, etc., just change the language unless their parents know the lingo. You can still *say* those words, but give it a quick explanation after you say it. For example, "when Krystal was passing free balls, (which was when I was tossing the high ball over the net to her...)." This makes it okay that not every parent knows volleyball, and you're educating the parent as well. Think about it: Do you want to show off your knowledge of volleyball terms, or do you want another lesson with this player?

- End with an invitation for more lessons (if that's what you want... if not, we'll talk about that more in chapter 20). You may feel comfortable asking for another lesson ("Today was fun, do you want to get together again next week at the same time?"). Or you may feel better about prompting them to ask for another lesson. I prefer to prompt, but I think it's up to you and your personality. A few examples of my favorite prompts are, "we had more setting drills to get to today, but we ran out of time," or "Jasmine looks like she'll be a great middle blocker, she just needs some more work on her timing and footwork." You're making it easy for them to ask for another lesson because they already know what they'd get! And this is why the entertainment portion is important... you want the player to ask for another lesson while you're there!

- Give homework. This will be discussed further in the following chapter, but I believe these extra assignments can make you stand out from other coaches.

- Get the money. This is either going to be an awkward handoff of a wad of cash, or you'll wait patiently while they write your name on a check. Give them payment information ahead of time to save yourself from this awkward pause if you care. Also, I suggest wearing something with pockets so you can collect the money and put it away. I've had 15-minute follow-up conversations while clutching $130 in my hand, and it felt a little odd.

That sounds like a lot of information, but you should be able to cover all the points in 2-3 minutes. It goes quickly because you're covering everything they'd ask about, so it's sort of a monologue in a way! I typically just get a lot of nods and smiles as I run through this part of the conversation.

## EXAMPLE OF A TYPICAL WRAP-UP

*"Hey Veronica, Katie did a great job today! I was really impressed with her serve and think she's got a lot of potential there. She was able to put a lot of power behind the ball, which most players her age tend to struggle with.*

*I also thought her passing form was pretty consistent, and she moved to the ball well. She did seem to struggle a little with those middle hits we were doing, but we could either move her to the outside or just focus on back-row attacks.*

*Footwork is always easy to practice at home, and the more she does it, the easier it will be in a game situation. Overall, I could really see her developing into a great back-row player with some more practice!"*

## WHY YOUR WRAP-UP IS IMPORTANT

It's highly likely that you gave your athlete a *lot* of feedback during your lesson. And it's possible (probable) that they will forget half of the things you worked on together, especially if you kept the session fast-paced.

By breaking down the lesson with the player and parent afterward, you're achieving six things:

- Emphasizing your value to the player as a coach.

- Giving the player and parent a chance to ask questions if something wasn't clear.

- Presenting the opportunity to schedule another lesson.

- Reminding the player of all the things they did well (especially important if they struggled with a skill towards the end).

- Reminding them that there's always more to work on.

- Building trust and confidence in you as a coach and a person.

I've seen coaches collect cash from the parents, tell the player "nice job," and then wave to them as they leave the gym. This isn't the worst thing you could do, but we can do better!

By holding yourself to a higher standard and giving families more than they expect, you can easily start to create a busy schedule full of private lessons.

# CHAPTER 17: HOMEWORK

Now, you don't *have* to do this, but parents will usually ask if there's something players can do at home to improve. If they have a ball, that opens up a lot of possibilities. But even without one, you can always recommend that they practice their footwork, arm swing, and visualization! You can also encourage general fitness like sprints, agility ladders, jump training, and even some endurance work.

There are quite a few drills players can do at home with just a ball and a wall. There are a ton of articles and videos online for this, so I won't go into too much detail, but there are options for every skill. I suggest you get creative and come up with your own ideas, too! This is what we're going to call "homework."

Telling your players how to practice at home increases the value of your lesson. If you have an extra minute or two after your lesson, you can even show the player and the parent what it is, what to look for, and maybe a phrase or two to keep in mind so they practice the skill correctly. I've also had parents record me while I demonstrated the skill I was telling the player to do at home, explaining what the focus was and how it would benefit them. If you're comfortable with that, parents *love* it!

Instead of just suggesting how to practice at home, you can also *assign* homework to players. Not everyone is as into this as you might expect. Still, nothing wrong with trying!

The next time you see the player, you can ask them about the homework. I usually only get about a 20-30% response that they did what I suggested, so don't expect everyone to go home and practice diligently.

For group lessons, you can also teach players drills they can do outside of the gym together. I will usually spend about 5-10 minutes in a lesson teaching the group a drill they can do at home.

The homework completion rate is usually higher with groups because it is more social and fun for the players to do together when they hang out. Examples include teaching young players how to pepper (when they pass-set-hit-repeat to each other) and pass-to-self competitions they can do.

# BENEFITS OF HOMEWORK

There are a lot of reasons for your players to practice volleyball after their lesson ends. By sharing these with your athletes and their parents, you'll increase the likelihood that they'll train at home. And as you're about to learn, this can help you in a number of ways.

Faster Progress:

More touches on the ball means faster learning. If a player is setting into a basketball hoop at home or passing to a taped-off spot on the wall, they're getting immediate feedback. The first attempt to set into the basketball hoop might be wildly off. The same goes for the second set. And the third set… but eventually, the ball *will* go in. And that brief moment of success encourages your athlete to continue practicing.

With enough practice, they may go from one set out of ten in the hoop, to four sets out of ten in the hoop. The form may not be perfect, and the accuracy surely has some room for improvement, but every time an athlete makes contact with the ball and gets feedback on whether it was "better" or "worse" for what they wanted to achieve, they are getting better overall.

Now armed with better control of their body and a better understanding of what they can make the ball do, your instruction is instantly more meaningful!

Giving players something to work on at home (by themselves or with a friend) makes your job much easier in the long run.

Better Value:

Let's face it... lessons are expensive. And even if a family has the means to sign up for lessons regularly, that doesn't mean they don't care about the value you provide them!

Giving players homework extends your impact on their son or daughter from the one hour you spend on court, to potentially 5+ hours of extra volleyball practice a week at home.

A parent or family member who sees their child practicing extra at home with the assignments you gave them instantly feels better about spending money on the lesson.

And if you feel bad about charging the market rate in your area, giving homework can help you justify a higher rate. Again, it's about value at the end of the day!

More Incentive To Continue Lessons:

Along the lines of my last point, giving homework to players encourages families to continue to sign up for lessons.

Parents enjoy providing the opportunity for their kids to get better, see progress, and pursue improvement. Especially when they feel like they're getting more than what they pay for.

## Stand Out From Other Coaches:

Many coaches will simply run a lesson and end the session, sending kids home until they see them again the following week. But if you are taking a few extra minutes to give instructions to the player on how they can practice at home, parents will notice!

It might not be immediate, though. In many cases, as long as a child is happy with their lesson, their parent will be, too. So, parents might sign their child up for lessons with another coach and stick with them indefinitely!

But over time, as you start to run more lessons and parents begin to discuss what their child is learning in those lessons, the topic of "homework" is sure to come up!

If other coaches in your area are not assigning homework, this is a tremendous advantage for you. As time goes on, you will likely become the coach that parents seek out. You go above and beyond, give more value, and that's what they want for their child!

## CHAPTER 17 TO-DO LIST:

Think of one or two at-home drills you could give to players for "homework" for each skill. Make sure to always have an option that does not include a ball, since not every player will have one. And always give the warning to the player that they need to ask their parents before they start at-home practice!

Bouncing a ball around in the house is a great way to break a TV, knock over fragile decor, and even break windows. By asking permission, the parents can at least get them set up in an ideal location.

# CHAPTER 18: GROUP LESSONS

This entire book is jam-packed with tips for you to build a schedule filled with private lessons. If executed properly, you'll create a steady flow of extra income on the side. In certain volleyball hotbeds and many metropolitan cities, you may even be able to make a living through coaching alone.

This would mean a busy evening and weekend schedule of private lessons, summer camps, and coaching during both the school and club seasons. You need to take coaching seriously if that's what you want to do, but just know that it's entirely possible. It is even more possible if you add in the real "money-maker."

Group lessons.

I know, I know, not everyone is reading this book to build up a profitable side-hustle. But if you are hoping to turn coaching into more of a career than a hobby, group lessons will certainly help you in that pursuit.

Beyond earning potential, group lessons offer several advantages for both coaches and their players over traditional one-on-one lessons. Here are a few benefits of running lessons with groups.

## A MORE EFFICIENT USE OF YOUR TIME

Working with two to three athletes at a time increases the number of athletes you can impact. Let's say you're running one-on-one lessons and dedicate three hours every Saturday morning to volleyball. At the end of those three hours, you'll have made an impact on three players. This is still great!

However, if you start to promote group lessons, you could have worked with at least six players during that time. On top of that, you would have had roughly the same impact on your players (more on that in the next section). If your goal is to impact the level of volleyball in your community, increasing the number of group lessons you run is a great way to do exactly that.

Think about it. You're spending the same amount of time out of your day, and getting to work with twice as many athletes, if not more. But you are not the only beneficiary when it comes to group lessons!

Your players will also benefit in a number of ways.

## MORE GAME-LIKE FOR YOUR ATHLETES

Let's imagine you're working with a sophomore athlete on her approach. She plays right side and needs more reps because she doesn't get set very often during practice. Then in games, she's caught off guard when she actually gets set and makes mistakes. This is pretty common for right side players, and I wouldn't be surprised if you get the opportunity to work with quite a few athletes in this same situation!

So, let's say she signs up for an individual lesson. She comes in and you start working together. You spend some time on her footwork, the angle of her approach, and now it's time to work on her contact. What do you do?

Well, since it's just you and her on the court, you're probably going to toss her some balls to hit, attempting to mimic the set. But there's a huge problem here. Actually, a couple of problems, if we're being honest!

For starters, tosses are *extremely* different from actual sets. The ball may end up in the same place, but the trajectory is a little different, and that can make a big impact... especially after a certain skill level is reached! Not only is the angle of the "set" not game-like, but your athlete will miss out on one of the most crucial aspects of perfecting her approach.

Timing.

In a game, no one is going to slap a ball for him or her, letting them know when to start their approach. Instead, they need to read the setter's body positioning and base their approach on the setter. Sure, the athlete may get better at hitting from a toss, and just through increased confidence will probably get better at hitting from a set. But the improvements are going to be minimal when you compare their progress against a player who practices hitting from an actual set.

And I know what you're thinking (because I've thought it too). "Maybe if I toss the ball to her to pass, I can set it to her to hit, and it'll be more game-like! Problem solved!"

Wrong... sorry!

Sure, the set is "better" than a toss. But anytime you insert yourself into the drill, you lose the ability to analyze and critique.

A second player there (preferably a player who wants to work on setting) creates incredible opportunities for you to teach the game. Your drill options increase dramatically once a second player is involved! In the example of the right side, now you can start to incorporate defense, quick sets, second ball over, transitioning… the list goes on and on! And that's before you even start thinking about any other skills!

There's a little more work and higher expectations in a group lesson, so you definitely have to bring your "A" game. But the payoff is worth it since their progress will be so much faster than in a one-on-one scenario.

## GROUP LESSONS SAVE FAMILIES MONEY

This is entirely dependent on how your pricing structure is set up. But most clubs and coaches who offer private lessons give a per-player discount if there are more players in the lesson. This is because your focus isn't entirely on the one player. But as mentioned in my previous point, the quality of the lesson is essentially the same (if not better) in a group lesson. What a deal!

Say you offer one-on-one lessons for $60 per hour. For a group of two players, you might charge $45 each. This saves the families money in the long run and makes budgeting for this extra expense a little easier.

So, if each player is paying $45, that means...

# YOU MAKE MORE MONEY

By running group lessons, you're able to turn your $60 per hour side-hustle into $90 per hour. And even though that may seem like "easy money," trust me, you've got to work for it!

When you run group lessons, there's an additional element of skill required on your part as the coach. Not only do you need to plan and run a high-paced, fun lesson which teaches skills at just the right level for each player, you also need to give feedback almost two to three times as much (you basically never stop talking), and make sure that each player is getting roughly the same amount of coaching and feedback.

Even though you're doing more work for less money per player, you're getting paid at a higher rate to keep things running smoothly. And although I believe a lesson with two players is the best possible group lesson, you may receive requests to run lessons with groups of three or four friends.

Even if you're only charging $35 per player, you could be making over $100 in an hour with groups. Spending just a few hours over the weekend could result in an extra $1,000 a month in your pocket. Not bad!

# PLAN BASED ON THE TYPE OF PLAYERS ATTENDING

A group lesson offers a ton of benefits… if it is planned properly! One of the key elements to running an efficient group lesson is that you have the *right* players attending with a shared goal in mind.

Let's do a recap of the types of players you will coach while running lessons:

- Players who want to get better
- Players who want to have fun
- Players who do not want to be there

When setting up group lessons, I highly recommend that you have an honest discussion with the parents about the type of players you will be working with.

Now, you don't want to directly ask, "does your player *actually* want to come to lessons?" But a quick discussion of their child's goals will offer clues as to what type of players you'll be coaching.

Do the parents mention that the players really want to make the 8th grade "A" team? You'll probably be working with teens who want to get better. Do the parents repeatedly say that the players "just need to get out of the house" and want to try volleyball? These players may not be totally sold on volleyball and might need a slower-paced lesson.

When you're scheduling a group lesson, it will be easiest to plan and run a lesson with players who want to improve and players who are there for fun. Now, it may be harder to get the "for fun" players to *focus*, but these lessons will still be successful if you keep the players moving.

If you feel you'll be working with players who aren't sure about volleyball or are nervous, be sure to come with plenty of drill options. A group lesson that includes this type of player could be very successful (they'll have fun with a friend and want to come back), or it could be a disaster. I've had siblings come in and fight the whole lesson because one wanted to get better, but the other was watching basketball on the adjacent court and had zero interest in volleyball.

Balancing a lesson when you have a player who is unsure about volleyball with another type of player can be a real challenge. You'll need to stay tuned into each player's attitude for the entire lesson. This can be mentally draining, but in the end, it's very rewarding if you're able to pull it off!

## DESIGNING YOUR GROUP LESSON PLAN

When two or more players are on the court, your

options really open up. Depending on the skill level of the players, their positions (if they have them), and just their general preferences can all influence how you set up your drills. There are two main drill styles that benefit players most in a group lesson. I like to classify these drills as "High-Rep" or "Combos."

# STYLE 1: HIGH-REP

You're going for fast-paced movement on the court, a lot of touches on the ball, and you're typically teaching only one skill at a time. This means all players will be running through the same type of skill in a similar manner.

One example would be to get in setting reps. You have one player set and go to the end of the line, while another player steps up to set. You keep it quick and work on the same skill with each player. This can include the same skill from the same position on the court, or the same skill performed from different positions on the court (think hitting outside and middle, passing left back and middle back, etc.).

Benefits:

High-rep drills make instruction easier, as your feedback to one player might apply to the other player(s). Another benefit is that you can focus on each player the entire time they are executing a skill.

Finally, these drills tend to move a little more quickly. Regardless of the skill, players will get more touches on the ball in a shorter amount of time.

Disadvantages:

With too many players in your group lesson, there might be too much standing around waiting for their turn. And if you don't have enough volleyballs, you might run out after a minute or two. You'll also run out of breath quickly when you're keeping the drills fast-paced... keep a water bottle nearby!

# STYLE 2: COMBOS

Combos are the main reason I promote group lessons. No matter what position combination you have, you can always find a way to combine the two to make your drills more game-like.

For example, let's say you have a back-row player and a setter. You could hit down balls (or toss free balls) to the passer, who then passes to the setter. The setter will work on setting to a target, or could even work on setting the back-row player for a back-row attack after a few progressions.

Viola! You've got a successful combo drill.

But what about a passer and a hitter? Easy! Maybe you want the hitter to work on controlling their hits down the line or cross-court. When you toss the ball, have the passer release into defense. Have the hitter focus on hitting in the direction of the passer, and you'll be working on the hitter's ball control. At the same time, the back-row player will get to work on reading the hitter and get some game-like reps. Have them attempt to pass to a target, and you've got a fun combo.

And what about a hitter and a setter? I'm sure you can come up with at least one idea, so I'll let you use your imagination to come up with more "combo" drill ideas.

Even if you have two hitters in a lesson, one could work on hitting while the other works on blocking or covering. Just think about how the two positions relate, and you can create a combo.

Benefits:

One of the most obvious benefits is that, instead of working from a toss or some other sort of controlled ball entry from the coach, you make the practice more game-like. Therefore, these types of lessons are more beneficial to your athletes!

Another benefit is that when there are two athletes, they've got an automatic practice buddy they can work with outside of the gym. Try to incorporate some sort of skill combo that players can work on without a net (I always teach younger players how to pepper if they don't know how to do that already) and you'll see their love for the game skyrocket!

Plus, when parents see their kids playing at home, or their child comes home and says they were playing volleyball with their friends at recess, they'll be happy to keep returning for lessons.

Disadvantages:

Although this is the best type of drill to run in a group lesson in my opinion, it does have its challenges. For example, if the players who come to you are at different skill levels, you might have a hard time running combo drills. Maybe a younger player can't get their serve over the net to start the serve/serve-receive combo you want to run, or the older sibling serves too hard for the younger one to be able to pass it up. When there's a large skill discrepancy, it might be best to limit the number of combo drills you use in your lesson plan.

## OVERALL

You will likely run your group lessons using a mixture of the two styles of drills. Notice which drills your players have more success with and try to use that type of drill more frequently with them!

# CHAPTER 19: FOLLOW-UP

Once I'm done with a lesson, I've found that following up with the family the next day is a great way to remind them of the skills we covered. Not only that, but this is an excellent way to get another lesson, too! Whether you prefer to send a text or email, either one is fine. But I've found there are different benefits offered by each method of follow-up.

In general, I prefer to send emails after a lesson if the parent is particularly interested in what their child needs to do to get better and if another lesson has not been scheduled yet. I also find these are a little more formal, so if you're working with someone new to you, an email might be preferred.

Text messages are much more casual, and I prefer texts when I've worked with families for at least two to three sessions. This is especially true when we have a standing weekly lesson or have already arranged a lesson at the end of our previous session.

I always like to confirm lessons with a quick text before I book the courts, because the drive home is usually when parents remember, "oh yeah, we're going to be out of town next week. I forgot to tell your coach!"

Each method of communication has benefits and disadvantages. To help you decide which form is best for you, I've listed a few tips and have written two examples of messages I might send after a lesson.

## EMAIL

Sending a quick email after a lesson is a great way to prove your value to parents and family members. When I send out emails, I like to include a few items every time to improve my chances of getting another lesson and be more helpful to my players!

First, I like to thank the parent for bringing their child to the lesson. Next, I'll include a brief recap of the lesson, which I've found is an amazing way to remind the family of your feedback. All you need to do is summarize your lesson review (from chapter 16). Finally, I'll end with a prompt for another lesson or ask for the lesson outright.

## Example follow-up email:

*Hi Stacy,*

*Thanks again for bringing Rebecca to our lesson yesterday. I had a lot of fun and hope she did too!*

*I just wanted to send a quick recap of our lesson for your records and for Rebecca to review:*

*What went well: Rebecca's serve is looking very strong for her age! Her form looks great, and the power is there. I think the next thing she'll want to focus on is developing her aim.*

*Areas for improvement: When we worked on defense, Rebecca was a little slow getting into position. This is okay though! With more practice on her footwork and work on reading the play, she'll move into position faster and will be ready for the hit. Once she can get into position sooner, her passing should improve dramatically. Encourage her to practice the footwork I showed her at the end of our lesson!*

*I'm free at the same time next week if you'd like to get together again for another lesson. Just let me know if you want me to schedule something and I'll get us a court reserved!*

*Thank you,*

*Whitney*

# TEXT MESSAGE

Text messages do not need to be very formal or even lengthy, but it is important to note that follow-up contact should always be made when you start working with someone new. If you decide to send a text, please be mindful of the time when you hit "send!"

I've noticed texting etiquette has deteriorated over the last few years, and I am personally annoyed by texts that come in too early or too late. Since this is just a formality and not urgent, I encourage you to only text families between 9am and 7pm.

Your text does not need to contain the amount of information an email would contain, but it should still touch on how the lesson went.

> *Hi Karen, I had a great time working with Brooklyn yesterday. Her hits were looking great by the end of the hour! Just wanted to confirm our lesson for next Monday at 6pm before I book the courts. Let me know. Thank you!*

If you're unsure which to use, an easy way to decide is to match the parent's preferred style. If they always email, I'll email. If they text, I'll text. Using the communication format that is easiest for them will win you points, even if it's not your preferred style.

# CHECKING IN BEFORE HOLIDAYS

Before holidays, long weekends, and school breaks, you can also reach out to see if families want to stick with the current schedule or if they'll be out of town. Better yet, you can suggest that they bring a friend or two along for a fun group lesson over the break!

Be sure to check in a week or two before holidays, since parents will often be extremely busy once these "breaks" arrive. The week or two before spring break is spent planning spring break, so this is when you want parents to know that you're available! Likewise, you do not want to interrupt family time over the winter holidays. If you have any availability in your schedule, let them know at the beginning of December.

Confirm that your normal gym will be open during these breaks before you book anything. Holidays are also a great time for facilities to shut down and resurface floors or clean.

# CHAPTER 19 TO-DO LIST:

Look at your calendar and see when the next school break is coming up. If you will be in town, make it a point to schedule a couple of lessons ahead of time!

Remember, check that the facility will be open and court space is available if you're planning to run lessons during any holiday.

# CHAPTER 20: "FIRING" ATHLETES AND PARENTS

Alright, you're ready to start running lessons! But before we wrap up, I wanted to point out one small detail that you should keep in mind when dealing with a particularly challenging parent, athlete, or family in general.

You can "fire" them.

What I'm trying to say is that if things aren't working out with a player, you do not need to continue giving lessons to them. Sure, it's hard to turn down an easy $40 for an hour of your time. But is it really worth it if you're getting berated throughout an entire lesson? Or constantly being asked for discounts by the same family over and over and over again?

I've experienced these situations, both directed at myself and other highly competent coaches that I've worked with. It's likely you'll have to deal with something like this, too! But I want to make sure you know that the issue likely isn't with you.

Sure, if you hear that the form you're teaching a player is different from what the high school coach is teaching, you should probably look into it. It's okay (and even encouraged) to reassess your methods if you get negative feedback! But if you're only hearing about problems from one or two families, I wouldn't take it personally.

There are people in this world who will complain about everything, and since you're organizing your own schedule now, guess what? You don't have to deal with it! I'm a big fan of minimizing stress in my life, and I have turned down lessons in the past for exactly this reason.

Typically, most of the issues stem from parents. Players are often very enthusiastic about lessons and will be super excited once we get on the court, which is why the parents will continue to try to schedule lessons with you (even if they're complaining the entire time). If your player is having a great time, they will keep asking their family to bring them back!

But if a dad or aunt is adding too much stress to your life, you have options. Before we talk about what you can do to deal with unhappy families, let's talk about what you *shouldn't* do.

# WHAT NOT TO DO

Ignore Them:

Trust me. On quite a few occasions, I've been tempted to ignore the text or email that comes in from these families asking for a lesson. When you're showing up and dealing with a negative family repeatedly, listening to their complaining isn't fun! But I definitely do not recommend ignoring them.

If you ignore them, they will continue to try and contact you. This could reflect poorly on you as a coach, because if this person is so negative towards you in person, imagine what they're willing to say to others behind your back! Most likely, they're going to tell people that you're not responding to them and share more of their negativity with anyone who will listen.

Or worse, they could go to your Director or supervisor, depending on what your role is in your organization. Then you're going to have to explain yourself, and it's not going to look like you're handling this conflict professionally.

Yell:

If certain players or parents are pushing your buttons, you need to deal with the situation before it gets to the point where you think you might lose your cool. Think about it. You could lose a ton of credibility in the parent's eyes, the player will probably be there and see it, and word will get around in your club and within your community. Not something you want to have happen!

And if you are working with a club, you could even end up losing your position. It doesn't matter how much a player or parent infuriates you, yelling isn't the answer. There are better ways to handle this situation.

Pretend To Be Busy:

I suggest avoiding this tactic because the truth is bound to come out eventually. Sure, you could let the parents know that you're busy and can't take a lesson with them. But this is short-term. They'll only call back or email and try to schedule something later on. If you just need a break from the family for a while, this could work. However, this is more of a band-aid than a real solution.

Those are the things that we don't want to do. Here are a couple of solutions you can use instead.

# POTENTIAL SOLUTIONS

Match Them With Another Coach:

My preferred solution? Give the lesson to another coach in your organization. I know that kind of sounds like you're just pushing the problem off to someone else. But depending on the size of your club, you probably have some other coaches who have different personalities than you!

I know that I work best with a certain type of player and a certain type of parent. Some of the individuals I've had a hard time working with actually got along much better with other coaches in past organizations. Suggesting another coach to work with is my preferred solution because you're actually *helping* the player more than if you were to continue giving them lessons yourself.

The player is going to continue to play and learn, and probably in an environment that's better for them than the one where you're always arguing with their parents. You're also helping another coach because you're sending a new lesson their way! Although it might be a little awkward to shuffle the player around, it will probably benefit everyone in the long run.

To do this, first approach the other coach and make

sure that they know the full story about why you want them to take on lessons with your current player.

Once they know the background information and have given you the "okay," you'll want to approach the parent and say something like this:

> *"Hi Susan, Abby's been doing a really good job with her training. Based on what I've seen, I think she has the potential to develop into a great middle blocker. Our other coach Jenny does a phenomenal job with our front-row players, and I wanted to recommend that Abby start working with Jenny.*
>
> *I think it would benefit her in the long run. I already spoke with Jenny about it, and her schedule lines up with our current schedule. Plus, she has other hours if you want more options. Is this something you might be interested in?"*

## Hold A Meeting:

If you're working with a difficult player or parent, I recommend holding a meeting with the parent and possibly with your Director or another supervisor in your organization. This is only if the player or parent is extremely disruptive. The point of this meeting is to address the poor behaviors you see in your lessons and to find a solution.

I want to point out that in my experience, it is

unlikely that their behavior will change after this meeting. But it's worth a shot! Explain what changes you hope to see from them in the future, and if they don't follow along with those expectations, let them know the consequences for continued misconduct. Ideally, these consequences are a part of your program rules. If not, be sure to agree with your organization on potential outcomes ahead of the meeting.

I highly recommend that you involve your Director in this meeting because it could impact the program. Quite honestly, this meeting could be the last straw and the family might decide to leave the club or program to find another organization. That's okay.

## Suggest Another Organization (AKA "Fire" Them):

If the family is not a good fit with you or any other coaches in your program, suggesting another organization that works better with their personality is a win-win situation, even if it doesn't feel like it in the moment. This is, effectively, "firing" the family. Frequently when someone is misbehaving, you can't necessarily "fire" them because it would negatively impact your organization. However, in extreme circumstances, it may be best to no longer allow them to participate in your programs.

I know it's not a super fun discussion to talk about

firing families. We don't want to hurt the player at the end of the day! So even if a parent is obnoxious or misbehaving, try to find a solution before you encourage them to find another place to play. But remember, you need to maintain your sanity! Otherwise, what's the point of coaching?

# CHAPTER 21: FINAL THOUGHTS AND ADVICE

Running lessons can be very fulfilling work for coaches who take the time to run them well. While no book can prepare you for every possible situation, by now you should feel confident in your ability to get started. Experience is the best teacher, and you will grow tremendously after you wrap-up your first session.

Now that you've finished the book, you're equipped with the knowledge to begin. But there is a huge difference between *knowing* what to do and *actually* doing it.

Taking action is often the hardest part of this process. Sorting through gym rental requirements and approaching families might deter you from starting. However, once you overcome those hurdles, you will feel a sense of happiness and contentment from making a difference.

To encourage you to take the leap and begin this new coaching experience, I've summarized ways you benefit from running private lessons. I also share why your athletes, their families, and your community ultimately *need* you to get started!

Let's start with you, shall we?

# COACH BENEFITS

Pushing Yourself:

Running private lessons is not for amateurs. To offer value to your athletes, you need to be on top of your game. You will consistently be challenged to do just a little more research and stay up-to-date with the latest techniques.

You will learn more about the tactics and strategies the local coaches are implementing with their teams, and you will be forced to learn new concepts that are outside of your comfort zone.

All of this amounts to you being a better coach at the end of the day. You will be constantly challenged to get better, and over the course of a season or two, the experience really adds up.

## Staying Active:

Most of us who coach have day jobs. And many of those day jobs involve sitting at a desk for long periods of time. We're constantly sitting. Sitting while we work, sitting in the car to and from work, sitting to relax once we get home... there's not a lot of time for exercise!

Coaching provides us with the benefit of activity. And when you're running a high-intensity private lesson, you can definitely work up a sweat! Not many people can get paid to get a workout in. This opportunity can be of real value to those of us who struggle to drag ourselves to the gym every couple of days.

## Building Positive Relationships:

It's obvious that you'll build relationships with your players. As you mentor them and guide them, you can't help but feel more connected to the athletes you work with. Their successes will become your successes, and that is an incredible bond to share.

Stepping back, we realize that we become close to parents, siblings, aunts, and uncles. These are the individuals who accompany our athletes to the gym, who cheer on the sideline, who ask for your advice and appreciate you working with their child. You may only run into them in the gym, but they can positively impact you.

Relationships that might not be as obvious are the ones forged with the people we interact with off the court. Building rapport with the front desk ladies while you wait for your lesson to arrive can brighten your day (and theirs, too). Getting to know the middle school coach or the club coach across town widens your network (and maybe helps land you a dream coaching job in the future).

We are fortunate to be in a position where we can make a positive impact on others, and we often receive that positivity back tenfold.

## Making Money:

How lucky are we that we can earn money to support ourselves and our families by playing a game?

It goes without saying that generating an income is a tremendous perk of running private lessons. Further, if you are in an area that supports it and you truly work at it, you can make a living through a mixture of coaching year-round and running private lessons.

## You Can Have Fun And Enjoy Your Work:

Probably the biggest motivator for me is the ability to have fun and enjoy what I do. While this book has focused heavily on the nuts and bolts of running private lessons, the real enjoyment comes from having fun on the court while teaching the next generation to play volleyball.

Lessons don't have to be so serious all the time. Sharing in funny moments as they're learning new skills is also fun to be a part of. Like when they swing at (and miss) the ball entirely because they're adjusting their timing.

Or when they try diving for the first time and just sort of flop on the ground. You can run high-level lessons and laugh, that's important to remember!

Ultimately, "fun" to me is watching my players develop their skills, gain confidence in their abilities, and become better athletes.

## ATHLETE BENEFITS

Skill Development:

In a one-on-one setting, or in small groups, players can get personalized attention that is often lacking in a team practice setting.

On a team, players are often held back in the areas where they excel and left behind in the skills they struggle with. Coaches lead teams as a whole, and will often try to strike the right balance of challenging athletes and being able to complete skills and drills successfully. This means that drills are conducted at "average" difficulty, rarely challenging the best players while athletes who struggle with certain skills fight just to get through the drill.

Lessons mean that you can take an athlete who is a strong passer, for example, and challenge them beyond what they would learn with their team. Likewise, if they have a hard time attacking, you can spend extra time on the basics to break down the skill for them. Again, this is something they wouldn't get the chance to experience in regular practices because coaches typically instruct at the "average" level, which would be beyond this player's abilities.

Knowledge Expansion:

When teammates aren't around, players often feel more comfortable asking questions. Whether it's skill-related or situational, they likely aren't asking their coach questions in practice unless they are very outgoing. This goes for camps as well, where it could be even *more* embarrassing to say that they don't understand something.

However, when it's just you and the player during a lesson, they don't have to worry about sounding stupid in front of their friends. You must treat *every* question as an excellent question because this will encourage the player to continue to ask for clarification.

The athlete starts to understand the game better because you are filling the gaps in their knowledge. You start to see the development of their "Volleyball IQ," and you get to watch as their confidence soars.

Volleyball IQ:

A lesson isn't just you barking instructions at the player. It's a conversation. This means they'll hear everything (instead of when they zone out in practice or poke each other in the huddle when their coach is talking), and therefore their understanding will go up.

You can spend 5 minutes giving them a ton of passing reps, instead of running a team through the same amount of reps in 15 minutes. That means you essentially get extra time to discuss strategy and teach them how to perform the skill in various situations.

Remember, as you fill in the information gaps, their on-court IQ skyrockets. Once they understand *why* they're supposed to stand in a certain spot on defense, and *why* they should send a free ball to a specific area of the court, you'll see them make better decisions based on the situation. This leads to the biggest benefit of private lessons, which is…

Confidence:

This one is huge and is easily the most significant benefit to players. When a player starts to put all of the puzzle pieces together, they walk into the gym a little taller, call the ball a little louder, and cheer for their teammates a little stronger.

Confidence comes from knowing what you're doing and understanding why you're doing it. As players develop their skillset, ask questions, and gain a better understanding of the game, this ultimately leads to more confidence on the court. In my opinion, this is the ultimate benefit of taking lessons. Eliminating (or at least reducing) self-doubt, strengthening their self-image, and improving their reaction time are all direct advantages of quality private lessons.

But players are not the only ones who benefit from private lessons! Families have something to gain, too!

## FAMILY BENEFITS

Closer Bonds:

Although not always the case, parents who sign their child up for private lessons are hoping to help their kid somehow. Maybe they're trying to help their daughter find a sport she loves or want their son to get better at volleyball so he can get more playing time with his team.

No matter the reason for private lessons, I've witnessed plenty of hugs, high-fives, and tons of smiles at the end of my sessions with these athletes. If you can successfully run a lesson for each player, you will see the player/parent bond grow.

If you have the opportunity to work with siblings, this is another way you get to help them grow closer together. Taking 10 minutes to teach sisters how to pass the ball back and forth, for example, leads to hours upon hours of peppering at home. Showing them mini-competitions they can do (i.e., who can pass the most in a row without dropping it) leads to even more hours spent together bonding while also building their skills.

And siblings don't have to be at the same level to play! Showing your 16-year-old libero how to teach their 10-year-old brother to pancake a ball ends up being a fun game they play when the 16-year-old has to babysit. Cousins have so much fun at lessons that they enter beach volleyball tournaments together. There are unlimited opportunities to encourage family bonds through private lessons.

Educating Families:

Not only are you fostering good feelings at the end of your lesson, but you're also teaching family members about the sport. I often think that we would have more fans of the sport if more people understood the game. Volleyball is an incredible sport, but it is confusing if you've never played before.

By conducting your post lesson wrap-up and by sending out follow-up information, you educate the parents and improve their experience of watching their child play. It is much more enjoyable to watch a game that you understand than to sit in the stands, wondering what is going on.

Remember, educating others isn't about showing off our knowledge. It is about taking complex concepts and making them simple to understand. You want parents to be able to leave the lesson with a solid understanding of what you taught their child so they can reinforce your instructions long after leaving the gym.

More To Talk About:

With greater understanding comes more to talk about, it's as simple as that.

When Mom has no idea why her daughter isn't getting more playing time, all there is to do is complain. The player may adopt this mindset and complain as well, or just get frustrated and tell her mom that she doesn't understand, closing down communication.

However, when Mom understands how rotations work and knows that her daughter plays a position that is front-row only, there's nothing to complain about anymore! Family conversations can now center around how great the player did hitting around the block or talking about making great attacking decisions at the net.

Or maybe another athlete really wants to serve in a match, but her Dad knows that means her passing needs to improve first. Now they spend weekends in the backyard working on passing to the homemade target he made. Better yet, they're mimicking what you did in your lesson, so you know they're getting quality touches on the ball.

Educating families has a more meaningful impact than just "knowing the rules." It can change family relationships in a positive way, and you can be the reason for that if you take the time to share your knowledge and explain yourself during these private lessons.

## COMMUNITY BENEFITS

Community Pride:

Growing up in a small town, I noticed that a considerable amount of "hometown pride" came from being associated with our top-performing sports. My high school was always sending wrestlers to state, we had great cross-country athletes, and we had a handful of top athletes in volleyball, football, softball, and baseball.

It's fun to go and cheer for teams who are winning. The atmosphere of a packed gym, the cheers after a monster play, and the feeling of victory at the end of the night… that's something that people want to be a part of.

Training athletes one-on-one won't immediately turn your local middle school or high school into a powerhouse. But it's a big step in the right direction!

Now, this an oversimplification of a long-term process, but follow along with me…

Once you start working with a player and they begin to play at a higher level, other players take notice. When Miranda starts to dominate the net in practice after a month of working with a coach on the weekends, her setter friend wants to tag along. Now the two of them are running plays and really connecting in matches, prompting other parents to remark on their improvements.

More parents reach out to you, and now you're working with a handful of players on the weekends when you've got time. The high school coach notices the difference you're making, and they start to run their own lessons as well. The younger players they work with begin to improve and "level up" the local competition.

You've created a culture where players and their families realize the benefits of these private lessons and small group sessions. Within two years, the level of play is higher across the board, and the high school program is winning 80% of their matches because of the higher skill level, better understanding of the game, and parent education.

Now the general public takes notice, and more people come out to watch. The students at the school start to feel like they're missing out and begin attending volleyball matches to be a part of the "winning" environment.

By the third year, the team is making it to state playoffs and possibly placing in the state tournament.

Because volleyball is so popular, clubs start to pop up in the area, and local rec programs begin running clinics and leagues for those who want a taste of the sport, but aren't ready for club.

This introductory level builds the overall skill level of all athletes. Four years ago, you'd be lucky to have a junior serving a tough topspin, but now 60% of JV is aggressively jump serving with relative success.

Your timeline may differ. The specific skills may differ. The potential for growth might be different based on your city's population. But this is more than possible. And you can be the one who starts it!

When I was in high school, my school often finished 3rd or 4th in our league, we would barely qualify for state playoffs, and we would usually lose in the first round. After I graduated and started coaching for a new club in the area, the skill level of local players grew tremendously. In my third year of coaching, I had an incredible 14u team that was mostly local girls.

Their senior year, they were the first volleyball team from my high school in over 30 years to win the state championship. I imagine this would have happened even faster if we had offered private lessons.

## KEY TAKEAWAYS

While this book is filled with specific actions for you to take and helpful tips as you begin to offer private lessons, there are a few overarching themes that I want you to keep in mind.

You're In The Entertainment Business:

I mentioned this throughout the book, but it really is one of the most important takeaways in my mind.

Once I realized this concept and used it to shape my decisions, I saw a tremendous amount of growth in my players and in the number of lessons I was giving.

Keeping players entertained means keeping players engaged in the lesson. When players are engaged in the lesson, they absorb the information. Absorbing information means they'll use what you've taught them, and they'll improve because of your instruction. Always give your lesson plan a once-over before you get to the gym and make sure it'll be fun.

Customization Is Key:

Sure, there are drills I run with every player I give a lesson to. But the way you customize those drills and make them work for each specific player who steps on your court... that's where the magic happens.

Let's take the basic example of teaching a player how to serve. Standing at the 10' line and warming up our arm by serving to each other seems pretty basic. But each player is different. For some players, I'll have them focus on how they shift their weight as they step. Older players working on their float serve will focus on the shape of their hand.

Always customize when you can, and don't do anything without a specific focus for that particular player.

## Flexibility Comes With Practice:

Maybe the parent told you over the phone that the player needed to work on serving, but then they arrive and say they want to work on passing. Would have been nice to know when you were planning the lesson, huh?

Don't worry, I make adjustments to nearly every lesson I run, and it gets much easier as you gain experience. Once you get a few lessons under your belt, you'll surprise yourself with the solutions you come up with!

Does a player want to work on passing instead of serving? No problem! You've got a previous lesson you ran with another player and can use that as a template. Did you forget your lesson plan at home? No worries! You now understand how the lesson is supposed to flow and can still run a good lesson without minute-by-minute detail.

If it feels tough at first, just know that it's normal. You will feel better with practice.

## Don't Overload:

When it comes to private lessons, there is such a thing as too much information! If you coach a team, you're probably accustomed to making constant corrections with your players and offering feedback to a new player with every other breath.

But when you've got only one player on the court, you need a different strategy. Telling your athlete that the steps are "right, left, right-left" for their approach, followed by stopping them and correcting the cadence/angle/speed after every single attempt is not going to work well.

If they ask? Sure, I'll make specific corrections. But they usually just need a couple of attempts on their own to get the hang of it. You don't want to let them continue using incorrect form for too long, but give them four to five tries before stepping in with corrections.

## Just Get Started:

The first lesson is the scariest. Navigating the setup process can be time-consuming and easy to delay until you're "less busy," choosing a time that works best for lessons can wait, and finally deciding to approach a parent to ask them for lessons... yikes! What if they say no? What if your price is too high? What if they laugh in your face?

I'll admit. They *might* say no. And your price *might* be too high for them... If anyone laughs, it'll be because they're thrilled you want to work with their child.

Whatever fears you have about getting started,

they're probably unfounded. I've discovered so much happiness in working with athletes in this setting. After I really found my groove, I was upset I didn't start sooner.

So, my ultimate piece of advice? Just get started, you'll be happy you did!

# CHAPTER 22: 10 DRILLS FOR PRIVATE LESSONS

Coaching in a one-on-one setting is very different than working with a team. For this reason, you may struggle to come up with drills when you plan your lesson!

To help you get started, I've included the top 10 drills that I use in practically every lesson I run. No matter what age or skill level you're working with, these drills are a great place to start to get your creative juices flowing!

You can always build upon these drills too, and possibly even combine them. For example, you might have your athlete serve to zones, run to their base position, and then transition into defense to pass to a target while you hit at them from a box.

The biggest obstacle that coaches face when

planning a private lesson is that they feel they need to get extremely creative when it comes to the drills they use. This couldn't be further from the truth. Stick with basic patterns that are frequently seen in play, and you'll be preparing your athletes to shine on the court.

Use the following key to read each drill:

- "X" = Player

- "C" = Coach

- Black lines show the path of the ball after a player makes contact.

- Lighter lines show player movement or the path of the ball a coach sends the ball in.

- The arrow shows the direction the ball or player moves in.

- The target is where a player is aiming to send the ball.

- The small circles indicate cones.

- The dark square with volleyballs indicates a ball cart.

- The light square indicates a box in some drills.

**"SERVE-TO-ME" PROGRESSIONS**

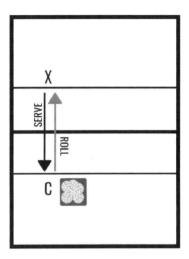

**Progression 1:** Player serves to coach from 10' line to 10' line. Coach rolls ball back to player to serve again or gives a new ball to the player.

**Progression 2:** Player and coach take a big step back after the player's arm starts to warm up. Continue to serve and move back every minute or so.

**Progression 3:** Once a player is beyond halfway, take the ball cart to the player and begin to instruct serve technique. Move back as appropriate.

# 2 SERVE DOWN THE LINE, SERVE CROSS-COURT

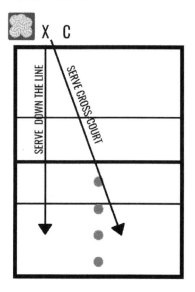

**Drill Setup:** Coach lays out cones to split court in half.

**Challenge #1:** Player serves down the line from their starting serving position.

**Challenge #2:** Player serves cross-court from their starting serving position.

*\*Younger players tend to move to serve "cross-court." Have them serve from the same spot every time to develop true "down the line" and "cross-court" serving skills.*

# SERVING ZONES

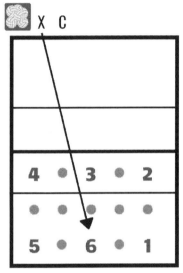

**Drill Setup:** Coach lays out cones to split court into 6 zones.

**Drill Description:** Explain zones to beginner athletes and teach them the hand signals. Start by having the player serve to zone 6. Follow with serving to zone 1 or zone 5. Finally, attempt serving short by serving to zones 2, 3, and 4.

#  TRANSITION AND PASS TO TARGET

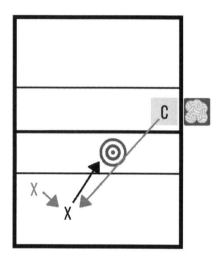

**Drill Setup:** Coach stands on a box with a ball cart next to them. Have a passing target (if available) setup in target range.

**Drill Description:** Player starts in back-row "base," the coach slaps the ball (indicating the set and the need to transition), and the player moves into defense to pass the hit to target.

**Add Variation:** Hit to the passer from different positions, or have the player pass from different positions.

# 5 OVERHAND BALL CONTROL

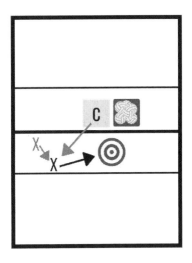

**Drill Setup:** Coach stands on a box with a ball cart next to them. Have a passing target (if available) setup in target range.

**Drill Description:** Player starts in front-row "base," the coach slaps the ball (indicating the set and the need to transition), and the player moves into defense to overhand pass a tip to target.

**Add Variation:** Toss free balls over to practice overhand passes from front-row.

# 6 SETTING TO TARGET

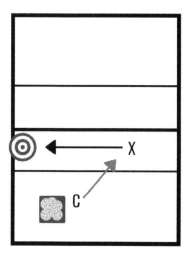

**Drill Setup:** Place your setting target in desired area.

**Drill Description:** Beginners may start in the setter's area, older players should transition from a defensive position. The coach will toss in front of the setter, who then sets towards the target. Start with a middle set for new or younger players.

**HOLD, DROP, AND SET**

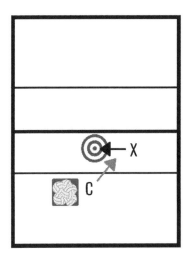

**Drill Setup:** Place your setting target in desired area. Player will start by holding a ball at their waist with their hands in "setting shape" around the ball.

**Drill Description:** The coach will slap another volleyball, indicating the player should drop the ball they are holding. This keeps their hands in "setting shape." They will then set the second ball to target. This works on proper hand shape while setting.

# 8 BACK-ROW ATTACKS

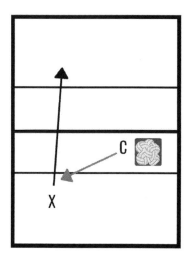

**Drill Setup:** Player will stand in the back-row as if they were in defense.

**Drill Description:** The coach will toss a high ball which should drop just on or behind the 10' line. Players will start by hitting down balls and work into back-row attacks.

**Add Variation:** Advanced players can hit into corners marked off with cones.

**3-STEP TO 2-STEP APPROACH**

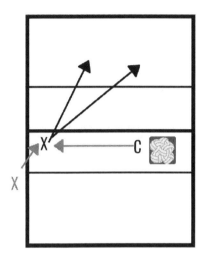

**Drill Setup:** Player will prepare to do a three-step (or four-step) approach.

**Drill Description:** The coach will toss a high ball mimicking a set to the player. As soon as the athlete makes contact, the coach will toss another set. The player must use a two-step approach from their location to hit the second set.

**"HITCHHIKER" & "TEATIME"**

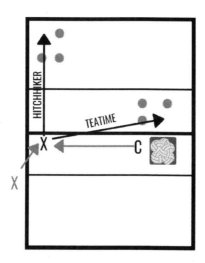

**Drill Setup:** Player will prepare to do a three-step (or four-step) approach.

**Drill Description:** The coach will toss a high ball mimicking a set to the player. First practice hitting down the line by finishing the swing with the player's thumb up (hitchhiker). Next, work on cutting the ball down the net by finishing the swing with the pinky up (teatime).

*\*Reverse the technique for a left-handed player.*

# ABOUT THE AUTHOR

Whitney Bartiuk is a volleyball coach, author of *Coaching Volleyball: A Survival Guide For Your First Season*, host of the Get The Pancake podcast, and creator of www.getthepancake.com.

She has trained players ranging from five-years-old to eighteen, and has worked with youth volleyball athletes in practically every setting you can think of!

Whitney has seen first-hand the impact a coach can have on an athlete through focused attention in a private lesson setting and hopes coaches use this book to build up the athletes in their communities.

Having coached in several states across the United States, Whitney is now living in Southern California.

She is working to grow her local volleyball programs while continuing to increase the number of resources available online for coaches through Get The Pancake.

Made in the USA
Middletown, DE
25 September 2023